T0391233

150 SPAS

YOU NEED TO VISIT BEFORE YOU DIE

By Devorah Lev-Tov

Lannoo

As our world becomes increasingly hectic and our lives become more stressful, the importance of self-care increases. Taking time for ourselves to unwind and actively heal our bodies, minds, and spirits is both bold and necessary. Spas are some of the best spaces for healing, relaxation, and self-care, and fortunately, the world has thousands of them.

From a solitary sauna concealed in the woods to an urban oasis soaring above a city's hustle and bustle, from a bathhouse harmoniously built around a naturally occurring thermal hot spring to a massive, state-of-the-art wellness center, the concept of what truly makes a spa a spa is wonderfully multifarious. A spa serves as a tranquil haven that shields you from the relentless demands of the outside world. It's a space dedicated to healing and rejuvenating your body and spirit, offering you the opportunity to pamper yourself, cater to your wellness needs and desires, and even experiment with the latest advancements in health technologies. But how does a spa accomplish its goal of helping you unwind, reset, and replenish your energy, and prepare to rejoin the world feeling revitalized?

Countless nations and cultures around the world have their own unique spa traditions, some of which trace back hundreds, and even thousands of years. Whether it's Icelandic thermal bathing, Nordic hot and cold contrast therapy, Hawaiian Lomi Lomi massage, South Korean beauty regiments, Japanese onsen soaking and shiatsu massage, Indian Ayurvedic principles and practices, traditional Chinese medicine, or Turkish and Moroccan hammam rituals —to name just a few—these diverse paths to the spa all share a common objective: rejuvenation and healing.

However you may choose to define the term "spa," it is indisputable that there are those that stand out among the rest. Below, you'll find a global list of the 150 spas that merit a visit before you die, be it for their exceptional design, opulence, historical significance, philosophical approach, size (large or small), location, expertise, or methodology. Regardless of your destination, I wish you rest and relaxation.

Devorah Lev-Tov

OVERVIEW

OVERVIEW

OVERVIEW

OVERVIEW

OCEANIA

01 THE SPA AT SANCTUARY CHOBE CHILWERO

Chobe National Park, Kasane, Botswana

TO VISIT
BEFORE YOU DIE
BECAUSE

Indulge in a lush African-inspired treatment amongst the trees of the bush.

Deep in the heart of the bush, at the edge of Chobe National Park, the riverside haven of Sanctuary Chobe Chilwero boasts the only full-service spa along the Botswana safari circuit—and it's a spectacular gem. Featuring a unique tree-top treatment room infused with African design and therapies influenced by local culture, you're in for an authentic and serene wilderness wellness experience. Using premium, organic Africology products crafted from African plants like rooibos, aloe ferox, and marula, alongside the luxurious French marine-based line by Thalgo, treatment options include the Soul of Africa Conditioning Body Massage and the Signature Salutation, a lavish treatment that uses antioxidant-filled rooibos and lavender mud culminating in a full-body massage. Post-treatment, immerse yourself in the split-level swimming pool area, complete with indoor spa bath, Vichy showers, and a relaxation area. While you bask in this serene atmosphere, keep an eye out for elephants, as this park is home to the world's largest remaining elephant population.

sanctuaryretreats.com/
botswana-lodges-chobe-chilwero-spa   +27 11 438 4650

02 SPA AT LA MAMOUNIA

Avenue Bab Jdid, 40040 Marrakesh, Morocco

TO VISIT
BEFORE YOU DIE
BECAUSE

This is one of the best of Morocco's legendary hammams.

Follow the lanterns down to the renowned Jacques Garcia-designed Spa at La Mamounia, a sanctuary in the heart of Marrakech honoring Moroccan culture and wellness practices. Here, there are three Moroccan hammams (two traditional and one private) adorned with colorful mosaic tiles and marble benches, making it a must to experience at least one. Hammam treatments begin with the application of a moisturizing blend of Moroccan black soap made from plant essences and olive paste (a nod to La Mamounia's 700-year-old olive trees). This is followed by a deep exfoliation using a Moroccan kessa exfoliating glove. The treatment continues with the healing powers of a ghassoul (mineral clay from the Atlas Mountains) body mask, made with local neroli and eucalyptus essences. Don't forget to set aside time for a leisurely swim in the famed indoor pool, an ode to Moroccan architecture with its marble columns, vibrant tilework, and painted ceiling.

mamounia.com/en/the-spa-wellness   +212 0524 388 600

03   SPA ROYAL MANSOUR

Rue Abou Abbas El Sebti, 40000 Marrakesh, Morocco

TO VISIT
BEFORE YOU DIE
BECAUSE

Traditional Moroccan therapies are combined with modern products for ultimate healing.

The heart of the Spa Royal Mansour is the pristine all-white atrium, where intricate lattice-work iron walls, crafted in the tradition of Moorish-style moucharabieh, cast fragmented light and create a play of patterned shadows. Ten marble and wood treatment rooms surround the atrium, while a glass-enclosed pool and traditional marble hammam are off to one side. The spa offers hammam treatments that include black soap wraps, ghassoul (mineral clay from the Atlas Mountains) treatments, kessa glove exfoliations, aromatic orange blossom soaps, relaxing steams, and floral waters.

In addition to these treatments, Spa Royal Mansour provides facials featuring Moroccan argan oil and skincare products from the Dr. Bergner line, marma massages, and watsu water therapy in the pool's hot basin. For those seeking a more holistic approach, several personalized wellness programs encompass everything from nutrition and fitness to therapeutic treatments guided by a professional consultant.

04

HOT SPA
AT BABYLONSTOREN

Klapmuts - Simondium Road, 7670 Simondium, South Africa

The combination
of farm-fresh
ingredients and
a hydrotherapy
area is perfection.

Set in the center of a sprawling farm estate, the Hot Spa at Babylonstoren harnesses the natural botanical riches of the South African landscape to craft a range of treatments that feature Babylonstoren's own unique blends of oils, balms, and lotions. The spa's bamboo pavilion is situated amidst tranquil greenery, and as a fully operational farm estate, Babylonstoren grows its own native aromatics onsite. From waterblommetjies and roses to clivia and fynbos, these botanical treasures are meticulously transformed into essential oils in the spa's own floral distillery, infusing their essence into the spa experience.

Beyond the pampering treatments, guests can tour the botanical fields and try their hand at creating their own handmade soaps and scrubs. The spa's centerpiece is the aqua area, which features a large pool and two circular vitality pools—one hot, one cold. These pools are connected by a narrow central pool, allowing you to leisurely swim between the contrasting temperatures. As you reach the mosaic-lined alcoves, allow the invigorating flow of ice-cold water to cascade over you before reveling in the sauna or salt room, meticulously crafted from raw pink Himalayan salt blocks. Babylonstoren recently introduced hammam and rasul treatment rooms, inspired by the traditions of ancient Arabian public baths.

babylonstoren.com/spa   +27 021 300 3929

05 THE WATERS OF ROYAL MALEWANE BUSH SPA AT ROYAL MALEWANE LODGE

F5J7+RM 1380 Amanda, South Africa

TO VISIT
BEFORE YOU DIE
BECAUSE

You can indulge in Africa's finest therapies while surrounded by the magnificent South African bushland.

Surrounded by the stunning landscapes of Greater Kruger National Park, the Waters of Royal Malewane Bush Spa is a true oasis. Guided by a philosophy rooted in the therapeutic properties of water, the spa treatments are enhanced by mineral-rich water sourced from an underground stream that flows through the reserve, then meticulously filtered through limestone and granite. For instance, the signature Royal Face and Body treatment begins with a luxurious full-body scrub in the African baths, followed by a body wrap. After that, there is an hour-long full-body massage, culminating in the rejuvenating African Essential Facial. The spa's three treatment rooms are positioned around the central courtyard, which features a heated lap pool. Additional facilities include a steam room, hot and cold African Baths, and four pre- and post-treatment casitas to relax in.

theroyalportfolio.com/
royal-malewane/wellness   +27 21 671 5502

06 THE SPA AT THE TWELVE APOSTLES HOTEL & SPA

Victoria Road, Camps Bay, 8005 Cape Town, South Africa

TO VISIT
BEFORE YOU DIE
BECAUSE

You can experience a massage in the salt-tinged air, surrounded by the breathtaking beauty of the ocean and mountains.

Perched at the very tip of the African continent, with Table Mountain as a majestic backdrop, the Twelve Apostles Hotel & Spa offers magnificent panoramic views of the Atlantic Ocean. The spa features a restorative indoor space, with seven elegant treatment rooms, a rasul chamber, hydrotherapy pool, plunge pool, a saltwater floatation pool, and a well-appointed relaxation lounge. For a truly indulgent experience, book one of two mountainside spa gazebos, where you can take in incredible vistas as you indulge in a treatment such as the Apostles Touch. This signature treatment includes a waterless scrub using calico bags infused with essential oils and fynbos, followed by a massage utilizing heated shells and stones, and a soothing scalp and foot massage. The spa uses a select range of products including Elemis and Tata Harper, along with B|Africa, a unique blend of indigenous African plant extracts and natural sea resources, utilized in all spas within the luxury Red Carnation Hotels group.

07   THE OCEAN SPA BVI

White Bay, Jost Van Dyke, British Virgin Islands

TO VISIT
BEFORE YOU DIE
BECAUSE

You can float amid
the cerulean waters
of the Caribbean
while receiving a
mindful massage.

Float your troubles away at one of the Caribbean's only floating spas, Ocean Spa BVI. Anchored in the turquoise waters of White Bay off the coast of Jost Van Dyke island, the spa is accessible by complimentary dinghy water taxi—or if you're feeling adventurous, you can boat, paddleboard, kayak, or swim there on your own.

Built primarily from salvaged lumber after Hurricane Irma in 2017, the floating wooden spa is a petite 550 square feet, but with salty ocean air and turquoise water in every direction, what else do you need? Best of all, rectangular windows under the massage tables allow you to gaze into the water and watch colorful fish swimming below during your treatment. Only one treatment is offered, but it more than satisfies: a seawater and herbal oil foot soak followed by a 60 or 90-minute massage, plus a rum cocktail.

08 FAIRMONT SPA BANFF SPRINGS

405 Spray Avenue, T1L 1J4 Banff, Alberta, Canada

TO VISIT
BEFORE YOU DIE
BECAUSE

It's a world-class spa set within a UNESCO World Heritage site and national park.

At the 40,000-square-foot Fairmont Spa Banff Springs overlooking the glacial Lake Louise, you can witness the sun's graceful descent behind the majestic Rockies while immersed in the outdoor whirlpool. Wrap yourself in a plush robe and bask in the tranquility of the spa terrace, or take a refreshing dip in the indoor mineral pool, and experience the invigorating sensation of cascading water in the three waterfall whirlpools, and relish the warm embrace of the eucalyptus-scented sauna and steam room.

Indulge in treatments such as the Signature Rockies Rehydration, which begins with a dry-brush exfoliation followed by the application of a rich mineral cream massaged into your skin, and culminates with a pampering face, scalp, neck, and foot massage. Alternatively, opt for the Glacial Reflections Facial, which features a rosehip tea and pine footbath, followed by a balancing rosehip facial massage, a moisturizing mask, and a temple and scalp treatment executed with glacial globes.

fairmont.com/banff-springs/
spa/the-fairmont-banff-springs-spa   +1 403 762 2211

09   MOUNTAIN TREK

3800 North Street,
V0G 1A0 Ainsworth, British Columbia, Canada

**TO VISIT
BEFORE YOU DIE
BECAUSE**

It's the perfect
destination for
a health reset in
the seclusion of
British Columbia's
wilderness.

Mountain Trek, honored as the most awarded health retreat in Canada, presents an exceptional weeklong immersive wellness program. The transformative experience encompasses sunrise yoga, daily hikes through the breathtaking British Columbia mountains, and invigorating treatments in the state-of-the-art spa overlooking a pristine mountain lake.

The spa facilities are a haven of relaxation, and include an infrared sauna, a steam room, an outdoor hot tub, and a refreshing hydrotherapy plunge pool. Your stay includes three therapeutic massages to further enhance your wellbeing. Those seeking a deeper level of rejuvenation have the option to add services like Biofield Tuning, a powerful version of sound therapy using vibrating tuning forks.

10   STE ANNE'S SPA

1009 Massey Road, K0K 2G0 Grafton, Ontario, Canada

TO VISIT
BEFORE YOU DIE
BECAUSE

The country castle makes an ideal setting for an accessible yet luxe spa retreat.

An all-inclusive spa retreat situated on 500 acres of Northumberland's rolling countryside just 90 minutes from Toronto, Ste Anne's Spa resides within an 1800s heritage fieldstone country castle. This destination takes pride in its customization, with everything meticulously crafted in-house, from delectable products at the gluten-free bakery to the organic Skin Nourishment skincare line used in treatments. Some of the spa's 35 treatments include a eucalyptus detox body wrap and reiki, and as a guest you also have access to numerous fitness and wellness classes. The spa's extensive facilities include four hydrotherapy pools of varying temperatures, a dry sauna, eucalyptus inhalation room, a steam room, a color therapy hot tub, and an outdoor spring-fed pool. Venture out and explore the miles of trails that meander through this expansive property, allowing you to work up a sweat amidst the natural beauty.

11   **BOTA BOTA**

Entrée McGill et, R. de la Commune O,
QC H2Y 2E2 Montréal, Quebec, Canada

You can revel
in a spa located
on a former ferry
boat, afloat on
Montreal's St.
Lawrence River.

This unique floating spa, at Montreal's Old Port on the St. Lawrence River, was once a working ferry boat before being transformed into a spa destination in 2010. The world of Bota Bota features numerous indoor and outdoor saunas, steam rooms, hot and cold tubs and showers, jetted baths, pools, and relaxation terraces and rooms spread across multiple decks for you to explore. Details such as a lavender-infused sauna, garden hammocks for lounging, and river access for a refreshing dip set this spa apart. Additionally, Bota Bota offers ten different massage therapies, from Lomi Lomi to cupping, ensuring you'll find exactly what your body craves. When hunger strikes, you don't need to leave: the on-board restaurant serves up local Quebecois ingredients in healthy, tasty preparations.

12   UMA SPA AT TIERRA CHILOÉ HOTEL & SPA

Sector, San José, Castro, Los Lagos, Chile

TO VISIT
BEFORE YOU DIE
BECAUSE

You'll experience
the abundance of
Patagonia in an
unforgettable way.

Most guests of Tierra Chiloé Hotel & Spa spend their days vigorously exploring the northern Patagonia region surrounding the boutique island hotel. These adventurous days are perfectly capped with a visit to the hotel's idyllic Uma Spa. Whether you're soaking in the heated outdoor infinity pool with stunning views of the surrounding Pullao wetlands, cocooning yourself in the seashell-like sauna and steam room, or exploring the full hydrotherapy circuit, your stress will melt away.

You can (and should) indulge in one of the spa's body and facial treatments that incorporate Chilean ingredients like hazelnut oil, maqui cream, and river stones. One notable treatment, the 80-minute Tierra Chiloé Ritual, features a body exfoliation with maqui exfoliant, followed by a wrap with thermal mud and maqui. To conclude, a massage with Chilean hazelnut and almond or coconut oil is performed while cold stones are placed on specific facial points, along with small stones on the spine and legs.

tierrachiloe.com/experience/spa-wellness   +562 6469 0518

13   WELLNESS SHALA AT FOUR SEASONS RESORT PENINSULA PAPAGAYO

26 Km al Norte del Doit Centre Liberia,
5000 Peninsula Papagayo, Carillo, Guanacaste, Costa Rica

TO VISIT
BEFORE YOU DIE
BECAUSE

This destination immerses you in the abundant nature of Costa Rica.

After an extensive renovation, the Four Seasons Resort Peninsula Papagayo has significantly invested in and expanded its spa and wellness offerings. Positioned high on the hills, the new Wellness Shala showcases a design rooted in bio-architecture and crafted by local artisans to create a sustainable structure inspired by the graceful flow and movements of the Guanacaste winds along the Pacific coast of Costa Rica. Treatments like the Signature Rainforest Massage draw from the surrounding Monteverde rainforest, utilizing its soothing sounds and the serenity of a peaceful river to guide the massage. The Volcanic Purification treatment, featuring a scrub made from volcanic ash followed by a volcanic mud mask, beautifully represents local landscapes and traditions. Sound baths, yoga sessions, and various other wellness experiences are also available.

14

VIDA MIA HEALING CENTER AND SPA AT THE RETREAT

Entrada de adoquín, Atenas, Barrio Jesús 700 metros Oeste de la entrada de Barroeta, Alajuela Province, Atenas, Costa Rica

TO VISIT
BEFORE YOU DIE
BECAUSE

The energy of the crystal mountain alone is worth experiencing.

Built on the slope of a quartz mountain overlooking the Pacific Ocean with stunning views of the Nicoya Peninsula, the Retreat Costa Rica is a secluded and exclusive wellness center that boasts its own organic gardens and coffee plantation. The Vida Mia Healing Center and Spa, designed according to feng shui principles (as was the entire resort), combines organic remedies with ancient therapies and the metaphysical powers of the four elements—earth, water, air and fire—to offer an extensive list of treatments. In addition to a robust menu of crystal healing therapies using a wide variety of gems, the spa provides acupuncture, Ayurvedic treatments, reiki, reflexology, Thai massage, and hydrotherapy bathing.

The Retreat grows and cultivates its own medicinal herbs, creating scrubs, tinctures, oil infusions, and creams, used in treatments like the Mini-Miracle Coffee Scrub. Between treatments and fitness and yoga classes, you can lounge on comfy couches, savor tea or biodynamic wine in the Gratitude Lounge Café and Tea Bar, reflect on the meditation deck, sunbathe by the Quiet Pool, or soak in the Jacuzzi and cold-water cascade.

15 NAYARA SPA AT NAYARA SPRINGS

21007 La Fortuna de San Carlos, Alajuela, Costa Rica

TO VISIT
BEFORE YOU DIE
BECAUSE

The allure of the volcanic jungle beckons, and you deserve to heed its call.

Prepare to be enveloped by the rainforest at Nayara Spa, an open-air tropical oasis within the adults-only Nayara Springs resort. Surrounded by lush jungle, you'll find yourself in the midst of nature's embrace. As you indulge in rejuvenating treatments, you'll be serenaded by a natural soundtrack provided by the local wildlife, including howler monkeys, toucans, frogs, and sloths who call this place home. You may even spot one of these enchanting creatures while you unwind.

The large menu of treatments incorporates local ingredients such as organic coffee, chocolate, and volcanic mud, which are expertly applied to your body, face, and scalp during the Nayara Signature Massage. Each treatment begins with a mineral foot soaking ritual, and each treatment room has its own private plunge pool where guests can luxuriate after a session. The carbon-neutral Nayara Springs offers complimentary daily morning yoga in an elevated outdoor pavilion overlooking the jungle canopy. The property also has pools fed by the volcanic hot springs, thanks to its location at the foothills of the impressive Volcan Arenal, which you can gaze at and admire from various vantage points across the property.

16 THE WELL AT HACIENDA ALTAGRACIA, AN AUBERGE RESORTS COLLECTION

Contiguo a la Escuela de Santa Teresa de Cajón, 11908 San José Province, Pérez Zeledón, Costa Rica

TO VISIT
BEFORE YOU DIE
BECAUSE

This is an amazing integrative wellness retreat in one of the most idyllic places on the planet.

Embark on a remote wellness retreat in the breathtaking mountains of Pérez Zeledón, known for its incredible biodiversity. THE WELL, an integrative, holistic wellness sanctuary originally established in New York City in 2019, opened its first international property in 2021 at the stunning Hacienda AltaGracia, an Auberge Resorts Collection. Spanning 180 acres of land, THE WELL boasts a generous 20,000 square feet of amenities, including eight treatment rooms, a hydrotherapy tub, thermal suite, and a healing garden. This unique destination showcases a diverse team of medical practitioners, health coaches, custom spa services, daily wellness programs, fitness and mindful movement sessions, and a calendar of seasonal retreats with visiting wellness experts. A highlight of your visit will be Casa de Agua, where you first select a robe from a curated collection, then apply purifying Costa Rican blue clay and recline on a heated marble stone bed before rinsing off in a powerful shower and then taking a dip in the tranquil pool. Don't miss the opportunity to partake in the Maderoterapia treatment, a signature holistic massage technique utilizing wooden tools to balance your energy and renew the lymphatic system. THE WELL also offers immersive wellness experiences that include a coffee scrub, followed by an herbal river bath and forest-bathing, culminating in an integrative crystal healing session.

aubergeresorts.com/altagracia/
wellness/the-well

+855 812 2212

17

THE SPA
AT CASA DE CAMPO

Carretera La Romana - Higuey Highway,
22000 La Romana, Dominican Republic

TO VISIT
BEFORE YOU DIE
BECAUSE

This brand-new spa is a luxe escape within an A-Lister's favorite resort.

The new Spa at Casa de Campo is an opulent wellness haven that combines indoor and outdoor facilities with cutting-edge technology. Its offerings include an extensive, state-of-the-art hydrothermal circuit, a Welnamis Aqua Wave Bed, and an MLX i3Dome for detoxing. What sets this spa apart are its treatments, which incorporate indigenous ingredients and methods, providing uniquely immersive cultural experiences.

Casa de Campo is a cherished destination for A-list celebrities, royalty, and heads of state, and it's no wonder. The Spa at Casa de Campo even offers a discreet "spa within a spa" for VIPs, groups and brides. These exclusive facilities feature a private entrance, comfortable lounge, dedicated treatment area, makeup station, dressing room, indoor and outdoor showers, personal vitality pool, and private bar with refreshments.

casadecampo.com.do/experiences/wellness   +1 866 818 4966

18 SUMAQ SPA AT PIKAIA LODGE

Sector El Camote a 100 m del Cerro Mesa,
200105 Santa Cruz, Galápagos, Ecuador

TO VISIT
BEFORE YOU DIE
BECAUSE

You can enjoy a massage in a bucket-list destination with unparalleled views to match.

What this spa lacks in size it makes up for in views and technique. The only five-star spa in the remote Galápagos Islands, Sumaq Spa is located in the only Relais & Châteaux hotel in the Galápagos.

Upon arrival, guests are greeted by an outdoor infinity pool overlooking the green highlands of Santa Cruz Island before entering the spa, which has an indoor-outdoor Jacuzzi, sauna, small locker room, and a double treatment room. This room has floor-to-ceiling windows overlooking the edge of a jaw-dropping, vegetation-filled crater, and the sounds of whistling wind and comforting music lull you into utter tranquility during your treatment. On the final day of your nature adventures around the islands, consider booking the Shamanic Signature Massage with Rosa, who will work lemongrass-scented oils into your skin with her magic hands and use Shamanic-inspired bamboo rain sticks that provide atmospheric sounds as she works them over your body.

19 FERN TREE SPA AT HALF MOON

Rose Hall, Montego Bay, St. James, Jamaica

TO VISIT
BEFORE YOU DIE
BECAUSE

This is one of the largest spas in the Caribbean offering overwater treatment bungalows.

Nestled between the sea and the majestic Montego Bay mountains, the Fern Tree Spa at Half Moon is surrounded by fragrant fruit trees and aromatic herbs. This vast 68,400-square-foot spa features 11 treatment rooms, two enchanting overwater cabanas, three separate pool areas, aromatherapy-infused steam and sauna rooms, an outdoor yoga pavilion hosting various movement classes, lush gardens, and a meditation labyrinth. Moreover, you'll find a tea room that offers tinctures made from the garden's own herbs, and a raw food café.

The spa's therapies combine indigenous ingredients and the best of international techniques. For instance, the Fern Tree Signature Massage indulges your senses with a cerasee foot soak, an herbal-infused rum splash, and the gentle sounds of a bamboo rain stick, while the Herbal Bush Bath offers a truly rejuvenating soak infused with the natural goodness of garden herbs.

20 ONE&ONLY SPA AT ONE&ONLY MANDARINA

Carretera Federal Libre 200 Tepic-Puerto Vallarta,
63724 El Monteón, Municipio de Compostela, Nayarit, Mexico

TO VISIT
BEFORE YOU DIE
BECAUSE

You'll find yourself amidst a verdant jungle setting with all the luxuries you can imagine.

Situated within the jungle paradise of the Riviera Nayarit coast, One&Only Mandarina offers an open-air spa that is simply breathtaking. The moment you step into the reception area and traverse a path of concrete stones over a reflecting pool, you'll be transported to a rainforest wellness wonderland. Here you'll find an adults-only pool, a temazcal heated dome for Mayan rituals, an outdoor mud bath area with showers, a separate building housing saunas and steam rooms, and a posh indoor-outdoor relaxation area. The spa's design is rooted in sacred geometry created by the Huicholes, an indigenous community of Riviera Nayarit. The layout is based on an eight-point star, representing the Huichol vision of spiritual regeneration, with each corner representing a different element: fire for the temazcal; water for wet areas; earth for the spa entrance; air and body for the treatment rooms; spirit for the ocean; mind for the equilibrium pavilion; and soul for the vitality area. Organic Tata Harper products are used for numerous facial and body treatments, including the signature Multi-Sensory Wellness Journey, while other standout treatments focus on Mayan culture, such as the Wirikuta Sacred Purification and Gemstone Healing Bliss.

oneandonlyresorts.com/
mandarina/experiences/spa   +52 327 689 0100

21

THE SPA
AT CHABLÉ YUCATÁN

Tablaje 642, San Antonio Chablé,
97816 Chocholá, Yucatán, Mexico

This may be the only spa in the world that overlooks a sacred cenote.

Set within 750 sprawling acres of jungle, the crown jewel of Chablé Yucatán is the 43,055-square-foot spa, uniquely positioned above a cenote (a natural limestone sinkhole held sacred by the Mayans). Thirteen wooden treatment cabins are suspended over the cenote, offering an unparalleled experience. The spa also features an outdoor spa pool made of petrified wood, an apothecary, a flotation tank, and a temazcal, a ceremonial Mayan sweat lodge. Among the range of Mayan-inspired treatments and rituals, there's an in-house Mayan spiritual leader who specializes in holistic healing, sacred ceremonies, and ancient feminine empowerment. The Signature Life Balance Ritual, for instance, includes a spiritual cleansing, a blessing of the four elements, a herbal salt and volcanic clay wrap, a precious stone energy-release massage, and a circle of life closing ceremony. You will exit the spa reborn.

22 SENSE, A ROSEWOOD SPA AT ROSEWOOD MAYAKOBA

Ctra. Federal Cancún-Playa del Carmen Km 298, 77710 Solidaridad, Quintana Roo, Mexico

TO VISIT
BEFORE YOU DIE
BECAUSE

This private island spa experience allows you to immerse in pure bliss amidst the Mexican Riviera, and emerge anew.

Set on a private spa island, Sense, A Rosewood Spa is enveloped by glassy lagoons and a lush mangrove forest within the Rosewood Mayakoba Resort. Your experience begins when you cross the bridge to the island and enter the Kuxtal Sensory Garden, which pays homage to the ancient beliefs of Mayan shamans, and provides many of the ingredients used in treatments. The spa offers a full hydrotherapy circuit, complete with cold plunge, Jacuzzi, steam room, and sauna. There's also a private yoga pavilion overlooking one of Mayakoba's cenotes, and an outdoor relaxation lounge. You'll find a dome-shaped temazcal (traditional Mayan sweat lodge), which is naturally heated with volcanic stones and scented with essential oils, offering a detoxifying steam led by the resort's resident shaman. For a full wellness experience, you can stay overnight on the spa island, where eight deluxe wellness suites offer wellness-focused amenities, including a personal meditation pavilion, a reflexology fountain, and in-shower aromatherapy.

23

THE SPA
AT RANCHO LA PUERTA

Carretera Mexicali-Tijuana Km 136.5,
21520 Rancho La Puerta, Tecate, Baja California, Mexico

TO VISIT
BEFORE YOU DIE
BECAUSE

Rancho La Puerta
is a pioneer in the
realm of wellness
retreats, with
decades of wisdom
and experience.

Rancho La Puerta is one of the original family-owned and operated fitness and spa resorts, opened in 1940 in Baja California. Situated on 4,000 private acres of gardens, mountains, and meadows, this retreat offers more than 80 fitness classes, including TRX, yoga, and Pilates, as well as 40 miles of rigorous hiking trails. The spa offers a comprehensive range of treatments and therapies from craniosacral therapy and acupuncture to Feldenkrais, reiki, and watsu. The spa experience is enriched with elements of local culture as seen in treatments like the cacao butter and sugar scrub, followed by a yogurt and honey mask, and a deeply indulgent cacao butter massage as offered in the Xocolatl Skin Replenishment.

rancholapuerta.com/spa-services   +1 800 443 7565

24   SPA MONTAGE LOS CABOS

Carretera Transpeninsular Km 12.5,
Int. Bahía Santa María, Twin Dolphin,
23450 Cabo San Lucas, Baja California Sur, Mexico

TO VISIT
BEFORE YOU DIE
BECAUSE

It's the only place where you can experience a rebirth inspired by whales.

At 40,000 square feet, Spa Montage Los Cabos is the largest spa in Baja. Drawing inspiration from traditional Mexican folklore centered around the Tree of Life, this spa weaves elements of the desert and local customs into its treatments. It also incorporates locally sourced ingredients such as the damiana plant, mango pulp, mezcal, and cacao to create one-of-a-kind experiences. One of the spa's most distinctive offerings is the Bathing with the Whales treatment, an immersive experience that unfolds in the spa's Serenity Pool, where you'll be harmoniously enveloped by the soothing sounds of whale songs. Therapists guide you through gentle movements designed to release blocked energy and facilitate a profound state of relaxation—a tribute to the majestic whales that migrate through Baja's Sea of Cortez each winter. In addition to the adults-only Serenity Pool, the luxurious spa facilities include steam rooms, jetted hot and cold plunge pools, and relaxation gardens.

25 KALLPA SPA AT TAMBO DEL INKA

Avenida Ferrocarril S/N, 08660 Sacred Valley, Urubamba, Peru

If you're hiking the Inca Trail, you absolutely deserve a rejuvenating reward.

Considered one of the best spas in the country, Kallpa Spa at Tambo del Inka, a Luxury Collection Resort, Valle Sagrado lies in the heart of Peru's Sacred Valley of the Incas, and the healing vibrations can be felt all around. Assuming you're here to visit Machu Picchu, you've probably done a fair amount of walking in thin air around uneven stones and your weary muscles are in dire need of revitalization, and the Kallpa Spa is here to provide just that. On offer is a wide variety of treatments based on ingredients from the Inca era, such as quinoa, passion fruit, coca, and even gold. Additionally, many of the ingredients are grown in the spa's large organic garden.

Make sure to leave ample time to adequately experience the thermal circuit, which includes hot and cold whirlpools with underwater beds and jets, steam and sauna rooms, and Vichy showers with adjustable pressures. There's also a beautiful heated indoor-outdoor infinity pool, enclosed by wood and glass, offering stunning views of the striking mountains.

marriott.com/en-us/hotels/
cuztl-tambo-del-inka-a-luxury-collection-
resort-and-spa-valle-sagrado/experiences   +51 8458 1777

26 SPA BOTÁNICO AT DORADO BEACH, A RITZ-CARLTON RESERVE

100 Dorado Beach Drive, 00646 Dorado, Puerto Rico

TO VISIT
BEFORE YOU DIE
BECAUSE

The custom-crafted botanical products used during treatments bring the Puerto Rican jungle to you.

Mirroring the lush beauty of Dorado Beach's natural surroundings, Spa Botánico seamlessly blends a magnificent natural environment inspired by ancestral Puerto Rican healing traditions, contemporary therapies, and the finest quality of local botanicals. And with internationally acclaimed architect Bill Bensley at the helm, renowned for cultivating sensual, imaginative and artistically striking landscapes, and the expertise of world-famous spa designers TLee Spas, it's not surprising that the five-acre spa is a sight to behold.

The Forbes Five Star spa is an ode to nature. It features ten private pavilions and two treehouse platforms situated amid the jungle canopy for a truly immersive treatment experience. An infinity reflection pool overlooks a picturesque pineapple garden, surrounded by verdant tropical gardens. Most treatments incorporate indigenous botanical ingredients, exemplified by the signature Manos Santas Ritual, which begins with a foot bath and consultation, followed by the application of custom-created bath salts, massage oil, and an herbal compress during a healing massage and bath in an outdoor stone tub surrounded by the sounds and smells of the tropics.

ritzcarlton.com/en/hotels/sjudo-dorado-beach-a-ritz-carlton-reserve/spa   +1 787 626 1100

27   QC NY SPA

Governors Island, Andes Road 112,
10004 New York, New York, USA

The Manhattan
skyline views from
the outdoor thermal
pool can't be beat.

When this thermal spa by Italian brand Terme came to New York, it set up
its extensive facilities inside a historic naval officers' building on Governors
Island, across the river from downtown Manhattan. To get there, you'll
take a ten-minute ferry ride from either Manhattan or Brooklyn, adding an
element of adventure. Inside, the multilevel space is filled with numerous
relaxation rooms, saunas, steam rooms, a Vichy shower, and various hydrotherapy experiences. However, the true magic of this spa is best experi-
enced on a beautiful day when you can fully indulge in the expansive outdoor heated pools, complete with an array of bubbling underwater lounge
chairs and massage jets. The highlight is the sweeping panoramic views of
the Manhattan skyline that you can savor from within the pool.
Day passes provide access to all the facilities, and you have the option to
enhance your visit with massages and other treatments.

28 SHIBUI SPA AT THE GREENWICH HOTEL

Greenwich Street 377, 10013 New York, New York, USA

The authentic Japanese design and techniques used here will undoubtedly unwind you.

As you step out of the elevator onto the lower level of the Greenwich Hotel, you are instantly transported to the heart of Japan. The dimly lit Shibui Spa immerses you in the culture, design, philosophy, and techniques inspired by the Land of the Rising Sun, making you forget you are in the bustling city of New York. Upon arrival, you'll be given a beautiful Japanese yukata robe to wear, setting the tone for your journey.

The lantern-lit indoor pool is surrounded by a 250-year-old wood and bamboo Japanese farmhouse, meticulously assembled using an ancient knot-tying technique by craftsmen brought from Japan. The walls were made using a traditional Japanese method that blends plaster and straw. The spa has five treatment rooms, including a traditional shiatsu room with a large tub for a variety of Japanese onsen bathing rituals. You can also indulge in massages like the Drunken Lotus, which utilizes hot, sake-soaked towels in long soothing strokes that's a perfect remedy for jet lag and reviving tired muscles. Experience traditional shiatsu performed on a tatami mat on the floor, or ashiatsu, a barefoot massage technique where therapists use wooden bars above the massage table to apply deep, consistent pressure with their feet and body weight.

thegreenwichhotel.com/shibui-spa   +1 646 203 0045

29 THE SPA AT THE RITZ-CARLTON NEW YORK, NOMAD

West 28th Street 25, 10001 New York, New York, USA

The Ritz-Carlton's newest location in New York's NoMad neighborhood, established in the summer of 2022, introduces a 6,800-square-foot spa, offering an ideal escape from the city's chaotic energy. The spa features eight treatment rooms and lavish men's and women's marble steam rooms and saunas. After your treatment, you can unwind in a small but serene relaxation room where you'll be served delicious cocoa tea.

The spa's treatments include Augustin Bader facials and Espa massages, including the signature Rose Quartz Remedy, which involves a full body exfoliation followed by a body and scalp massage, with the use of frangipani, rose geranium, and palmerosa oils, along with rose quartz stones employed in a similar fashion to hot stones.

ritzcarlton.com/en/hotels/
nycro-the-ritz-carlton-new-york-nomad/spa   +1 212 404 8430

30　SHOU SUGI BAN HOUSE

Montauk Highway 337, 11976 Water Mill, New York, USA

This is a serene
Japanese-style
oasis in one of the
wealthiest enclaves
in the United States.

Simplicity and minimalism are the guiding principles at this upscale
Hamptons wellness destination that embraces Japanese traditions of wellbeing and style. The retreat emphasizes health and wellness, with the
spa and healing barn as its focal points. Look out for strategically placed
healing crystals throughout the well-manicured property. The spa houses
a thermal area complete with a watsu pool, saunas, and plunge pools at
varying temperatures for contrast therapy. It also features five treatment
rooms for therapies such as the Clear the Path hybrid massage that draws
from Eastern and Western techniques, algae body wraps, and Biologique
Recherche facials. The healing barn is where you'll enjoy sound baths, reiki, and twice daily classes such as yoga and meditation.
The spa provides three meals a day by Danish chef Mads Refslund (former-
ly of Noma), highlighting local and seasonal ingredients. If you're staying
overnight in one of the cottages, you'll be treated to a nightly bath in a
traditional hinoki wood soaking tub with salts and herbs.

shousugibanhouse.com　　　　+1 631 500 9049

31   SPA BY EQUINOX

Hudson Yards 31, 10001 New York, New York, USA

The medical spa industry is evolving and this one is at the top of the science-backed spa chain.

Towering above Manhattan's swirling traffic, Spa by Equinox, located within the first (and as of now, only) hotel and spa by the luxury fitness center brand, focuses on cutting-edge, science-backed medical spa treatments. The results-driven spa menu is tailored to enhance both inner and outer wellbeing through innovative treatments, including the Icoone Roboderm, a noninvasive lymphatic body-sculpting device designed to reduce cellulite, firm the skin, relieve muscle tension and soreness, and promote digestion and overall gut health. Additionally, there's the Gold Collagen Facial, created in collaboration with renowned plastic surgeon, Dr. Lara Devgan, and the spa's latest offering, the MLX i3 Dome by Gharieni. This technology utilizes Far Infrared Rays technology to stimulate the body's metabolism and induce sweat production, coupled with a Plasma and Light Therapy face device that rejuvenates the skin and supports detoxification.

Conclude your spa experience in one of the relaxation pods, where you can unwind with views of the Hudson River views while receiving an IV drip from NutriDrip. These drips offer a selection of vitamin and serum combinations ranging from energy-boosting to skin-enhancing formulas.

32   SPA TOWN AT PAWS UP

Paws Up Road 40060, 59823 Greenough, Montana, USA

How often can you get a top-notch spa treatment inside a tent and still feel lavish?

As you approach the spa area of this sprawling luxury ranch resort tucked into the Montana forest, you'll encounter a quaint wooden cabin that serves as the check-in area and a semi-circle of glamping-style tents surrounding a lush meadow alive with wildflowers in spring and summer and dotted with grazing horses all year round. These tents also serve as treatment rooms, offering a sense of adventure without sacrificing luxury as you relax on a plush massage table.

The spa's treatments are inspired by Native American rituals and ingredients, and incorporate locally sourced components such as rocks from the nearby Blackfoot River to enhance the experience. Mother Nature provides the soundscape with the sounds of a gurgling brook, chirping birds, and rustling breezes. Additionally, this spa has a delightful feature—massages for pets, complimentary with any 60-minute human spa service.

pawsup.com/spa   +1 877 588 6783

33 LIFE IN BALANCE SPA AT MIRAVAL ARIZONA

East Vía Estancia Miraval 5000, 85739 Tucson, Arizona, USA

TO VISIT
BEFORE YOU DIE
BECAUSE

This legendary retreat is a grand dame of the Arizona wellness resorts.

Known for its comprehensive wellness retreats, Miraval Arizona is the original original—and many say best—of the three Miraval resorts. It's located on the edge of the Sonoran Desert, surrounded by iconic saguaro cacti and striking red mountains.

The Life in Balance Spa offers an extensive menu of services that draws from global cultures, including Tibet, India, Europe, China, and more. From reiki healing to Gua Sha facials and the Brahmi Swedna—an Ayurvedic full-body treatment incorporating warm oil, steamed poultices, a ghee foot massage, and an aromatic linen wrap—the spa has a treatment for everyone. In this desert oasis, you can experience treatments in petite cabins outdoors, allowing you to savor the caress of the desert air.

The spa facilities include an outdoor pool overlooking the desert, an outdoor hot tub, saunas and steam rooms, and a spacious relaxation area with indoor and outdoor sections. Beyond the spa, the resort offers a wealth of wellness activities, including fitness classes, meditation workshops, nutrition classes and consultations, equine therapy, and much more. Miraval Arizona is the ideal destination for a transformative mind and body experience with a lasting impact on your life.

miravalresorts.com/
arizona/life-in-balance-spa

+1 520 825 4000

34 THE SPA AT MOHONK MOUNTAIN HOUSE

Mountain Rest Road 1000, 12561 New Paltz, New York, USA

TO VISIT
BEFORE YOU DIE
BECAUSE

This enduring lakefront spa places mindfulness at the forefront of all its wellness offerings.

In 2023, the 144-year-old family-owned landmark, Mohonk Mountain House, unveiled a refreshed 30,000-square-foot spa that includes a seasonal outdoor treatment gazebo with views of the glistening lake and surrounding Shawangunk cliffs. Guests can book treatments or private meditation sessions in this beautiful setting. Dr. Nina Smiley, meditation and mindfulness expert, leads some of these sessions, contributing her calming voice to excellent effect.

Indoors, a light-filled solarium awaits, complete with a cozy fireplace and comfy lounge chairs where you can relax before or after your treatment. The spa offers the Contrast Hydrotherapy Massage, which simulates the sensation of a bracing lake dip by combining hot and cold showers, a revitalizing scrub, and an invigorating massage. Additional spa facilities include steam and sauna rooms, and there are a variety of fitness classes and meditation sessions that are included with your stay at the hotel.

mohonk.com/spa   +1 877 877 2664

35 THE SPA AT FOUR SEASONS HOTEL PHILADELPHIA

North 19th Street 1, 19103 Philadelphia, Pennsylvania, USA

TO VISIT
BEFORE YOU DIE
BECAUSE

This spa will introduce you to the mystical healing powers of crystals high above the city.

The Four Seasons Hotel Philadelphia occupies the top 12 floors of the Norman Foster-designed 60-story Comcast Center, making it the highest situated hotel in North America. The spa, located on the 57th floor, is the city's first and only Forbes Five Star Spa and it's accompanied by a mirrored indoor infinity pool that provides a surreal sensation of swimming amidst the clouds. One unique feature is the incorporation of over 700 pounds of healing crystals into the structure of the spa's walls, with each treatment room named after a specific type of crystal.

Signature treatments include the Crystal Oil Massage, which involves a full-body massage using crystal-infused oils, and the Luminous Crystal Facial, featuring rose quartz, carnelian, and aventurine crystals. For a truly memorable experience, you can reserve the Night Spa, where you will be treated to an array of candles and signature Jeff Leatham floral arrangements by the infinity pool. This is followed by a couples massage, private swimming amidst the city's twinkling lights, and concludes with Champagne and pastries.

36 TIERRA SANTA HEALING HOUSE AT FAENA HOTEL MIAMI BEACH

Collins Avenue 3201, 33140 Miami Beach, Florida, USA

TO VISIT
BEFORE YOU DIE
BECAUSE

The flamboyant design still provides a soothing sanctuary in the Magic City.

One of the most beautiful and colorful spas in Miami, the Tierra Santa Healing House offers both a visual feat and an oasis of calm. The 22,000-square-foot spa is renowned for its beauty and skincare offerings, as well as its holistic healing arts. Collaborating with esteemed brands such as Naturopathica and Biologique Recherche, the spa provides a comprehensive wellness menu.

For an exclusive and enchanting experience, reserve the Hammam Rose Ritual, an indulgent treatment that begins with an invigorating lemongrass-and-mimosa scrub on the spa's heated hexagonal Amazonite stone, followed by a restorative mask of volcanic clay and calendula. The treatment culminates with a jasmine-scented steam session and a calming rose-oil body massage. The hammam is part of an extensive wet zone, which includes a waterfall, an herbal steam room, a dry sauna, an ice room, and a tepidarium with heated stone beds.

faena.com/miami-beach/
wellness/tierra-santa-healing-house   +1 786 655 5570

37   MII AMO

Boynton Canyon Road 525, 86336 Sedona, Arizona, USA

This legendary
spa amid Sedona's
red rocks exudes
a healing energy
all its own.

Tucked away in Sedona's quintessential Boynton Canyon, Mii amo has been a source of inspiration over the last two decades for guests seeking a deep connection with nature and holistic wellbeing. Guests can embark on all-inclusive retreats lasting three, four, seven, or ten nights. Following a significant renovation, this Relais & Châteaux property now features a two-story movement and fitness studio, a dedicated consultation wing, and expanded wellness facilities.

Skincare enthusiasts will appreciate the use of Babor products, while spa services incorporate sound and light therapy, CBD oil, and hot and cold stone treatments. Mii amo integrates Eastern and Native American techniques into many of its offerings, with a minimum treatment duration of 75 blissful minutes, administered by intuitive therapists.

38 FOUR SEASONS RESORT MAUI AT WAILEA

Wailea Alanui Drive 3900, 96753 Kihei, Maui, Hawai'i, USA

TO VISIT
BEFORE YOU DIE
BECAUSE

Enjoy a Hawaiian Lomi Lomi massage by the ocean, in the very place where this ancient practice originated.

Situated in the tropical paradise of Wailea, the Spa at Four Seasons Resort Maui is where the switched-on come to switch off. Drawing inspiration from Maui's rich cultural heritage, the spa offers Hawaiian-inspired massages, body treatments, and facials. Traditional Hawaiian Lomi Lomi massages employ ancient techniques to restore balance, while body treatments infused with local ingredients like coconut and volcanic clay leave the skin nourished. To truly immerse yourself in paradise, opt for these treatments in one of the three oceanfront, open-air *hales* (thatched-roof houses), with breathtaking views of the Pacific and the gentle lapping of waves as a peaceful soundtrack.

For a more contemporary approach, the spa also offers an exclusive white-glove wellness service in partnership with Next|Health, featuring customized IV therapy treatments, including an exclusive new sleep IV, vitamin shots, and biomarker testing.

fourseasons.com/maui/spa   +1 808 874 8000

39 BAMFORD WELLNESS SPA AT 1 HOTEL HANALEI BAY

Ka Huku Road 5520, Princeville, Kauai, Hawai'i, USA

TO VISIT
BEFORE YOU DIE
BECAUSE

This is a brand new, state-of-the-art spa on Hawai'i's Garden Isle.

This sustainable, nature and wellness-focused island oasis overlooking Kauai's North Shore opened its doors in 2023. The resort's expansive wellness center offers a diverse menu of services and techniques through its spa, fitness center, medical spa, and retreat center. Carole Bamford, organic pioneer and founder of the Bamford skincare and spa brand, helped create the natural-wood, 18,000-square-foot spa, which provides an open, serene setting for wellness and mindfulness sessions and therapies. Expertly crafted body treatments, inspired by local Hawaiian culture, feature specially formulated products made from Hawaiian medicinal plants and organic ingredients, such as tulsi, noni leaf, coffee, sea salt, and honey. The spa offers six rituals designed to address various needs, such as sleep, herbal healing, and recovery, as well as a wide selection of massages, facials, and body treatments. The cutting-edge facilities and amenities include 18 treatment rooms, a quartz bed, an aqua table, a cryotherapy chamber, a hyperbaric chamber, infrared saunas with halotherapy, Dreampod ice baths, a Somadome meditation pod, and a salt pod flotation chamber.

1hotels.com/hanalei-bay/
do/bamford-wellness-spa

+1 808 977 1230

40

SENSEI LANAI, A FOUR SEASONS RESORT

Keomoku Highway 1, 96763 Lanai City, Hawai'i, USA

TO VISIT
BEFORE YOU DIE
BECAUSE

This island oasis takes you on a customized wellness journey with all the trimmings.

A luxurious wellness enclave set within the pine-covered mountains of the island of Lanai, Sensei Lanai, A Four Seasons Resort is the ultimate adults-only wellness experience. You'll embark on a personalized journey led by your Sensei guide, who will curate a bespoke itinerary complete with spa treatments, fitness and wellbeing classes, and consultations. The spa's 10 hales are luxurious, Japanese-inspired sanctuaries of tranquility, each featuring a Japanese ofuro bathtub, an infrared sauna, indoor and outdoor showers, oversized massage tables, private plunge pools, and comfortable lounging areas. A highlight of the experience is the new Thermal Body Mapping, an exclusive Sensei-developed thermographic technology that creates a visual map of the body to reveal asymmetries, muscle tightness, and potential areas of discomfort.

41 CASTLE HOT SPRINGS

North Castle Hot Springs Road,
85342 Morristown, Arizona, USA

TO VISIT
BEFORE YOU DIE
BECAUSE

The mineral-rich
hot springs are
mindfully woven
into the spa
experience here.

In the heart of Castle Hot Springs, a historic wellness destination amid peaceful desert surroundings, are mineral-rich hot springs, which are seamlessly integrated into every aspect of this immersive resort. The hot springs' water is rich in lithium, magnesium, and bicarbonates and it's incorporated into all spa treatments, whether it's a spritz to initiate treatments, a relaxing pre-soak, or a personalized watsu treatment, where the therapist joins you in the water. Spa treatments also feature the therapeutic waters in scrubs and wraps, as well as the use of fresh herbs and plants cultivated on the property's farm or sourced locally. Start your day with yoga and tai chi classes, followed by a mineral soaking circuit, and then engage in a wide range of outdoor activities that call for pre-and post-soaks in the beneficial hot springs to assure both peak performance and complete recovery.

42 FAIRMONT SPA AT FAIRMONT CENTURY PLAZA

Avenue of the Stars 2025, 90067 Los Angeles, California, USA

TO VISIT
BEFORE YOU DIE
BECAUSE

This state-of-the-art spa is a favorite among celebrities for a good reason.

The 14,000-square-foot masterpiece Forbes Five Star-awarded spa at the Fairmont Century Plaza in La La Land fuses ancient movement modalities with state-of-the-art equipment, offering a menu of celebrity-loved treatments. Designed by Yabu Pushelberg, the posh spa exudes minimalist luxury, with soft lighting accentuating slate-colored tile, high ceilings, warm woods, sleek black accents, and natural polished gray stone. You'll find nine treatment rooms, experiential rain showers, sanariums, aromatherapy steam rooms, a Himalayan salt room, and a hammam. The spa offers an extensive range of performance-driven facials, relief and recovery massages, and sensory mood-enhancing body treatments. A state-of-the-art biohacking treatment is also available, incorporating an anti-gravity chair; a HigherDose Mat that uses magnetic field therapy, heat, and healing crystals; NormaTech lymphatic drain boots; a NuCalm disc; and a binaural meditation session, promising the effects of a six-hour power nap in just 30 minutes.

fairmontcenturyplaza.com/wellness/   +1 310 424 3032

43 THE RANCH MALIBU

Cotharin Road 12220, 90265 Malibu, California, USA

It's the place to kickstart your health, and maybe spot a Hollywood A-Lister in the process.

Nestled amidst the scenic Santa Monica Mountains and spanning 200 acres of rugged coastline, The Ranch Malibu is a wellness retreat renowned for delivering real results. It offers structured shared wellness programs with a minimum stay of six nights, accommodating a limited number of 25 guests, as well as private wellness experiences. A typical day includes a four-hour group hiking excursion, followed by lunch, nap time, an afternoon strength-training class, restorative yoga, and a daily massage. Organic, plant-based group meals focus on detoxification and are known for their low-calorie offerings. Additionally, the retreat provides a variety of health services and treatments, such as IV therapy, cholesterol testing, energy healing, and access to infrared and cryotherapy saunas.

44   SPA SOLAGE AT SOLAGE, AN AUBERGE RESORT

Silverado Trail North 755, 94515 Calistoga, California, USA

TO VISIT
BEFORE YOU DIE
BECAUSE

You should experience the healing properties of Calistoga's mud and water in a luxurious setting.

Napa Valley's charming town of Calistoga is known for its wineries, ranches, and natural hot springs that produce mineral-rich mud. At Solage, an Auberge Resort, the 20,000-square-foot Spa Solage takes full advantage of its surroundings. The open-air spa incorporates the famous Calistoga mud and mineral water in various therapies. The centerpiece, the Bathhouse, features multiple geothermal pools with temperatures ranging from icy cold to a comforting 98°F, and a warm 103°F. A must-try treatment is the signature Mudslide, a modern twist on the traditional Calistoga mud bath. This detoxifying treatment includes a mud bath customized with your choice of pure essential oils, followed by a soak in a private tub filled with geothermal mineral waters. The experience culminates with relaxation in a state-of-the-art sound chair, where healing from harmonic music resonates through your body.

aubergeresorts.com/solage/wellness/spa   +1 855 790 6023

45   SPA PALMERA AT THE BOCA RATON

Est Camino Real 501, 33432 Boca Raton, Florida, USA

TO VISIT
BEFORE YOU DIE
BECAUSE

The opportunity to indulge in a wellness experience in this palatial setting is an unforgettable experience.

Awarded Five Stars by Forbes Travel Guide, Spa Palmera is a sprawling 50,000-square-foot retreat at the Boca Raton, inspired by the magnificent Alhambra Palace in Spain. The extravagant spa boasts elaborate mosaics, grand arches, and a courtyard surrounded by lush gardens. Its extensive amenities include 44 treatment rooms, waterfall whirlpools, and a private pool. The Alhambra's influence is woven throughout the spa experience, from the sparkling infused strawberry-mint-rose water welcome drink to the royal-inspired ritual baths, which serve as the backdrop for various hydrotherapy treatments. Notable treatments include the Diamond Facial by Natura Bisse and the Alhambra Body Ritual, featuring a dry brush, mandarin and jasmine body polish, citrus body wrap, and full-body massage. The spa also houses the biostation, offering cutting-edge anti-aging and wellness services like IV therapy, in-depth diagnostic testing, hormone restoration, peptide therapy, and more.

46

THE SPA AT THE OMNI GROVE PARK INN

Macon Avenue 290, 28804 Asheville, North Carolina, USA

TO VISIT
BEFORE YOU DIE
BECAUSE

This may be the largest cave spa in the world, offering a magical subterranean experience.

Surrounded by the scenic Blue Ridge Mountains, the Spa at the Omni Grove Park Inn boasts a 43,000-square-foot subterranean spa within the historic hotel. This grotto-like structure is adorned with rock walls, arches, and tunnels, housing an array of water features, including mineral-based pools, therapeutic waterfall pools, and a lap pool adorned with 6,500 fiber-optic twinkling stars and underwater music. Amenities also include men's and women's contrast pools, inhalation rooms, saunas and eucalyptus-infused steam rooms, an outdoor whirlpool, three fireside lounges, and a spa café. The robust treatment menu offers everything from traditional massages and facials to unique experiences like wellness pod sessions with infrared heat and aura photography and readings, followed by chakra-enhancing treatments.

omnihotels.com/
hotels/asheville-grove-park/spa   +1 800 438 5800

47 CAL-A-VIE HEALTH SPA

Spa Havens Way 29402, 92084 Vista, California, USA

TO VISIT
BEFORE YOU DIE
BECAUSE

You'll enjoy a
holistic wellness
retreat in an
environment
reminiscent of
a French chateau.

Owned by the Haven family since 2000, Cal-a-Vie offers an escape to the essence of France right in Southern California. The property boasts historic French buildings, including a 1615 chapel, 1710 greenhouse, and a 1715 parish house, all transported from Dijon. These structures, along with the meticulously landscaped gardens and vineyards, create an authentic French countryside atmosphere that transports guests to another world. The retreat's spa and wellness packages offer everything from yoga, meditation, and mindfulness workshops to fitness and nutrition consultations. Spa therapies are equally diverse, focusing on vinotherapy using local grapes and incorporating Eastern-inspired treatments like bamboo massages, Gua Sha, Thai massage, and cupping therapy. The staff's certified experts include an acupuncturist, a chiropractor, and a naturopathic doctor, who provide immune boosters, hydrating IVs, and weight-loss enhancers.

48 PANGOLIN SPA AT DUNTON HOT SPRINGS

Road 38 8532, 81323 Dolores, Colorado, USA

These historic cabins are home to a top-notch hot springs retreat.

Set in the heart of Colorado's San Juan Mountains, Dunton Hot Springs, a former mining town turned Relais & Châteaux resort, is renowned for its remote location and its namesake natural hot springs. These natural hot springs, featuring calcium bicarbonate with a strong concentration of dissolved iron, manganese, and a touch of lithium, have a rich history dating back to the Ute Indians. Today, guests at Dunton Hot Springs can enjoy the benefits of this natural wonder in five ways: inside the restored 19th-century bathhouse, under the starry sky at the source, in the pool outside the bathhouse, in the pool behind the Dunton Store cabin, and within the cozy Pangolin Spa cabin. After a soak, indulge in alpine-inspired treatments at the spa, including herbal poultice massages and ashiatsu barefoot massages. The spa also offers complimentary yoga and fitness classes, private nutritional counseling, sound baths, and professional wellness workshops.

49 HOT SPRINGS SPA AT THE OMNI HOMESTEAD RESORT

Sam Snead Highway 7696, 24445 Hot Springs, Virginia, USA

You can soak in the same mineral-rich waters that once welcomed Franklin Roosevelt and John F. Kennedy.

This historic Virginia resort, frequented by presidents, dignitaries, and Native Americans for thousands of years, features mineral-rich hot springs. Recently, a 14-month, $4 million rehabilitation brought its historic pools into the modern era. The original octagonal stone basin, built in 1761, is a testament to its rich history. Alongside the two historic octagon-shaped bathhouses, the Aqua Thermal Suite offers experiential showers, an herbal cocoon experience, thermal heated loungers, a cold cabin, and an aromatic steam room. The Serenity Spa Garden boasts European-inspired gardens, outdoor spring-fed pools, and plush cabanas for lounging. The reflexology walk stimulates the feet in the flowing waters of the mineral spring. The sunlit spa offers a wide-ranging menu of body treatments and facials featuring the mineral-rich spring water.

omnihotels.com/hotels/
homestead-virginia/spa

+1 800 838 1766

50   THE SPA AT INNS OF AURORA

Sherwood Road 700, 13026 Aurora, New York, USA

TO VISIT
BEFORE YOU DIE
BECAUSE

This is where lakeside bliss, luxurious comfort, and world-class art converge.

Set on 350 acres of rolling farmland in New York State's Finger Lakes region, the Spa at Inns of Aurora resides in a trio of interconnected barns. With panoramic views of Cayuga Lake, the spa is adorned with 50 pieces of exceptional modern art, personally curated by the owner. Its impressive facilities include ten treatment rooms, four outdoor hydrotherapy circuit spa pools, an indoor hot spa pool and cold plunge, multiple indoor saunas and steam rooms, an outdoor sauna pavilion, a salon with a manicure/pedicure room, and an indoor/outdoor lounge boasting expansive lake views, fireplaces, and an outdoor firepit. The spa's treatment menu focuses on mind, spirit, and body, offering treatments like Abhyanga massage, reiki, and the Red Flower Hammam Ritual. Post-treatment, explore one of the nature trails surrounding the spa.

51 THE SPA OF THE FIVE GRACES AT THE INN OF THE FIVE GRACES

East De Vargas Street 150, 87501 Santa Fe, New Mexico, USA

TO VISIT
BEFORE YOU DIE
BECAUSE

The spa's one-of-a-kind art and décor create an inspiring and calming environment.

The Spa of the Give Graces offers a mystical and immersive Santa Fe experience. Upon entering the original adobe doorway you are instantly transported to an art-filled haven. Craftmanship and textiles sourced from Central and Southeast Asia, along with stunning mosaics handmade by the owner, create a unique atmosphere. The spa has five treatment rooms featuring original adobe walls, *kiva* clay fireplaces, mosaic-tiled skylights, and intricately carved wooden panels. Treatments are Ayurvedic-inspired, including the Himalayan Salt Stone Massage, which features heated Himalayan salt stones and flower and herb-based oils. Your journey begins and ends with the soothing resonance of Tibetan metal cymbals. The lounge is an oasis of calm with a mosaic-tiled fountain and gigantic crystals, while the outdoor space offers carved wooden lounge chairs covered in Indian textiles surrounding a pool, sauna, and hot tub.

fivegraces.com/spa-wellness

+1 505 992 0957

52 THE SPA AT TEN THOUSAND WAVES

Ten Thousand Waves Way 21,
87501 Santa Fe, New Mexico, USA

TO VISIT
BEFORE YOU DIE
BECAUSE

You can experience the Sante Fe mountain hot springs in a truly distinctive manner.

Situated between downtown Sante Fe and a national forest, Ten Thousand Waves is a Japanese-inspired mountain hot spring spa. Whether you're a day spa guest or staying overnight in one of the 16 rooms fashioned after a Japanese ryokan, you can reserve one of seven private hot tub suites accommodating up to ten people. Each suite offers a unique experience with a hot tub, sauna, and some including a cold plunge. The larger Grand Bath is reserved exclusively for spa and hotel guests. As a spa guest, you can indulge in traditional Japanese massages and facials, including shiatsu and a Japanese organic massage facial. Craving a snack? The izakaya serves delectable Japanese treats.

53 THE SPA AT OJO CALIENTE

Los Banos Drive 50, 87549 Ojo Caliente, New Mexico, USA

New Mexico's natural, curative riches are put to excellent use here.

Ojo Caliente, situated amidst the stunning landscapes of New Mexico, taps into the state's abundant natural resources with sulfur-free hot springs emerging between desert cliffs and cottonwood forests. These springs contain arsenic, lithia, soda, and iron, and the spa is built around these healing waters. Ojo Caliente offers nine communal hot springs and numerous private hot tubs with *kiva* fireplaces. The spa treatments incorporate the mineral-rich waters along with local herbs and plants, and every treatment features their signature herbal infused hot towels. The hot stone massage employs hand-gathered basalt rocks, while sound healing sessions uses tuning forks to create harmonic vibrations on chakra points. To fully immerse your body in the local abundance, try the Blue Corn, Prickly Pear, Sea Salt Scrub with Hot Oil Hair Therapy, which utilizes heritage blue cornmeal and sea salt as a scrub, along with prickly pear for skin nourishment. A hot coconut oil hair treatment and wrap infused with rosemary, eucalyptus, and peppermint complete this refreshing scrub.

54 LAKEHOUSE SPA AT LAKE AUSTIN SPA RESORT

River Bend 12611, 78732 Austin, Texas, USA

TO VISIT BEFORE YOU DIE BECAUSE

With over 100 unique treatments, you're guaranteed to emerge renewed and revitalized.

Located alongside a placid lake in the rolling knolls of Texas Hill Country, the Lake Austin Spa Resort is a calming escape just 30 minutes from Austin. The 25,000-square-foot LakeHouse Spa boasts 30 treatment areas, including garden tents and suites, an outdoor Palm Pool, a hot tub, cabanas, an indoor Junior Olympic-length lap pool in the Pool Barn, the Aster Café featuring ingredients from on-site gardens, and two acres of terraced foliage and aquatic gardens. The spa's menu comprises over 100 massage, body, and skincare treatments and therapies grounded in principles like aromatherapy, Ayurveda, hydrotherapy, Moortherapy, and thalassotherapy. The renowned AquaStretch Myofascial Release treatment offers incredible pain relief, combining an assisted stretching session with manual pressure in a warm pool.

lakeaustin.com/spa   +1 512 372 7380

55   AMAN SPA AT AMANGIRI

Kayenta Road 1, 84741 Canyon Point, Utah, USA

TO VISIT
BEFORE YOU DIE
BECAUSE

You'll experience luxury amidst the jaw-dropping landscapes of a desert canyon.

Stretching over 25,000 square feet across the rugged Utah desert and its canyons, the Aman Spa at Amangiri provides a sensory journey inspired by Navajo traditions, Ayurveda, and traditional Chinese medicine. The spa menu features Grounding, Purifying, and Nourishing massages, facials, body polishes and wraps, which draw on the elements of earth, wind, fire and water. You can also try the Desert Calm treatment, featuring a body wrap with red Sedona clay and a signature Oxygen Facial. The indoor-outdoor spa includes a water pavilion with a steam room, sauna, plunge pool and heated step pool, a flotation pavilion with a private relaxation area, a finishing salon, and a Pilates and yoga studio. Additionally, the adjacent Camp Sarika offers two spa suites with uninterrupted desert views.

56 BANYAN TREE SPA RINGHA AT BANYAN TREE RINGHA

Hong Po Village, 674400 Jian Tang Town, Shangri-La County, Diqing Tibetan Autonomous Prefecture, Yunnan Province, China

TO VISIT BEFORE YOU DIE BECAUSE

After trekking in the Himalayas, you deserve a deluxe spa experience that honors local traditions.

Set in the Tibetan Shangri-La highlands and surrounded by the Himalayan mountains, the Banyan Tree Ringha resort is built from traditional Tibetan farmhouses, providing a secluded mountain retreat. Banyan Tree Spa Ringha, located within an original farmhouse structure, is designed with traditional Tibetan textiles, wood carvings, and pottery, offering a cozy sanctuary for relaxation after exploring the Himalayan peaks. Spa treatments draw inspiration from traditional Himalayan practices and the ancient Chinese Five Elements philosophy. For an authentic experience, try the Sense of Place Ringha Relief to harness the best of locally sourced ingredients, via an herbal steam, a pearl barley body scrub, a gui shi hot stone massage, and a red rice ginseng body conditioner with pouch application. Afterwards, savor local yak butter and ginger tea in the comfy relaxation room.

banyantree.com/china/ringha   +86 887 828 8822

57 UR SPA AT THE PUXUAN HOTEL AND SPA

Wangfujing Street 1, 100006 Dongcheng District, Beijing, China

It will have you embarking on a journey to the dark side, but expect it to be captivating and restorative.

Hidden away from the Forbidden City and Beijing's bustling commercial district, the PuXuan Hotel and Spa offers a posh retreat. The deluxe UR SPA is spread over two floors, featuring nine treatment rooms, two scrub rooms, a couple's suite, plus a dedicated foot therapy lounge. Unlike many spas with lighter color palettes, UR SPA's tones are black and gray, creating an environment that effectively isolates guests from the outside world. You can begin your spa experience with a warming and energizing scrub on heated marble beds in a dedicated scrub room, followed by a massage or facial. Post treatment, you can visit the movement studio, where a trainer offers personalized yoga practices, or simply retire to one of the indoor or outdoor quiet zones.

thepuxuan.com/en/
beijing-luxury-puxuan-hotel-spa   +86 10 5393 6688

58 CAPELLA WELLNESS AT CAPELLA TUFU BAY

Tufu Resort Area, 572000 Yingzhou Town,
Lingshui County, Hainan Province, China

TO VISIT
BEFORE YOU DIE
BECAUSE

It's a beautiful
exploration of how
celestial rhythms
affect wellness.

Capella Tufu Bay, located on the tropical southern coast of Hainan Island, is a design marvel by renowned architects Jean-Michel Gathy and Bill Bensley. Its Capella Wellness spa is a gorgeous refuge that fuses ancient Eastern traditions with modern therapies and beauty rituals, all guided by the cycles of the moon. During the waning moon, cleansing treatments are recommended for deeper effects, while the waxing moon is the time to nourish yourself and refocus your energy. The spa features a hammam and snow cabin, offering respite from Hainan's tropical climate. Sleep pods, cabanas, vitality pools, a thermal suite, a swimming pool, and an outdoor tai chi area provide additional relaxation areas.

capellahotels.com/en/capella-sanya/wellness   +86 898 8309 9999

59

THE AMAN SPA AT AMANDAYAN

Shishan Road 29, 674199 Gucheng District, Lijiang Shi Yunnan Sheng, China

TO VISIT
BEFORE YOU DIE
BECAUSE

This spa provides an authentic experience of traditional Chinese medicine at its source.

Set within the hilltop haven of Amandayan, the Aman Spa is housed in wooden pavilions surrounding a 66-foot-long outdoor heated swimming pool. The spa's menu draws on local healing traditions, traditional Chinese medicine, and China's abundance of medicinal herbs. Therapies range from seasonal baths and scrubs using local ingredients to Chinese foot reflexology and tui na, a form of massage that works to relax the body and restore the flow of qi (life force) by focusing on specific acupressure points. Signature treatments include the Bamboo Aromatherapy Massage where heated bamboo sticks are used as an extension of the therapist's hands, and the Herbal Compress Massage, which uses prai root, ginger, turmeric, and lemongrass to improve circulation and soothe muscles. There are four self-contained double treatment rooms with private steam showers, wooden bathtubs, and relaxation areas, plus two private hydrotherapy rooms for scrubs, baths and wraps. Private fitness, tai chi, yoga, Pilates, and meditation sessions are available in the gym and the movement studio.

aman.com/resorts/amandayan   +86 888 533 9999

60 ASAYA HONG KONG AT ROSEWOOD HONG KONG

Salisbury Road 18, Tsim Sha Tsui, Kowloon, Hong Kong

TO VISIT
BEFORE YOU DIE
BECAUSE

This is a true urban oasis in the sky that zeros in on your personal needs.

Situated on the sixth and seventh floors of the Rosewood Hong Kong building, Asaya is the first urban outpost of the luxury hotel brand's innovative and integrative wellness concept. Asaya Hong Kong offers alternative therapies, lifestyle coaching, educational wellness programming, fitness, and an array of healing treatments. Specialized treatments include the Well-Women series in partnership with Resorting Mums, which supports women in their fertility journey with five signature treatments. There is also an in-depth mindfulness menu, offering meditation, hypnosis, and art therapy. Facilities include 11 treatment rooms, an outdoor infinity pool with panoramic harbor views, and two special Asaya Lodges, offering accommodation that combines Rosewood brand luxury with wellness amenities. In these extraordinary rooms, everything is curated to your needs, based on a consultation with Asaya's resident doctor of naturopathy.

rosewoodhotels.com/en/
hong-kong/wellness/asaya

+852 3891 8888

61 PENINSULA SPA & WELLNESS CENTER AT THE PENINSULA HONG KONG

Salisbury Road, Tsim Sha Tsui, Kowloon, Hong Kong

TO VISIT
BEFORE YOU DIE
BECAUSE

It combines modern luxury and traditional elements for a true wellness journey.

The Peninsula Hong Kong, known as the legendary Grande Dame of the Far East, boasts a spa that blends traditional Chinese elements with contemporary flair. The opulent design combines marble, rustic woods, woven textiles, and textured granite. The lavishly appointed 14 treatment rooms, hammam-style steam rooms, saunas, aromatherapy showers, and cooling ice fountains offer plenty of places to escape. The stunning Roman-style indoor pool features intricately carved marble columns and floor-to-ceiling windows overlooking Victoria Harbour and Hong Kong's skyline.

Signature treatments to indulge in include the Qi Balancing Meridian Massage, a therapeutic Chinese acupressure massage, and the Life Lived Best Sensorial Journey, which stimulates all five senses over two hours. All Peninsula hotels, this one included, have incorporated the brand's new Life Lived Best wellness program, which offers access to a dedicated wellness portal, round-the-clock wellness concierge services, special wellness activities, and healthy dining options.

peninsula.com/en/
hong-kong/wellness/luxury-hotel-spa   +852 2696 6682

62 THE SPA AT ANANDA IN THE HIMALAYAS

The Palace Estate, 249175 Narendra Nagar, Uttarakhand, India

TO VISIT
BEFORE YOU DIE
BECAUSE

In the birthplace of Ayurvedic medicine, you'll have an immersive experience of this ancient practice.

Ananda in the Himalayas is a luxury wellness retreat on a palace estate secluded on the foothills of the majestic mountains, near the spiritual town of Rishikesh and the holy Ganges River. Guided by the principles of Ayurveda, yoga, and Vedanta philosophy, Ananda offers an array of wellness retreats from Ayurvedic Rejuvenation to Stress Management. The 24,000-square-foot, three-level spa features wet areas, 24 treatment rooms, private aromatic baths and showers, Finnish saunas, Turkish steam baths, plunge pools, and footbath areas. Treatments include abhyanga (four-handed massage using sesame oil), pinda sweda (application of herbal poultices), shirodhara (oil poured in a stream on the forehead), acupuncture, cupping, reiki, Thai massage, and a long list of scrubs, wraps, and facials using local ingredients.

63 THE SPA AT THE LEELA PALACE UDAIPUR

Lake Pichola, 313001 Udaipur, Rajasthan, India

You can live like Mewar royalty in a dazzling lakefront setting.

The magnificent Leela Palace Udaipur on the shores of Lake Pichola, with the Aravalli Mountains in the background, promises an exquisite royal experience. You'll also relax like royalty in the tented spa, set beside a fragrant guava orchard. Alongside a 160-year-old Shiv temple and haveli mansion are yoga and meditation tents as well as eight Rajasthani-style luxury treatment tents, adorned with opulent linens and silk, private plunge pools, and some with soaking tubs.

The spa's extensive amenities encompass a salon, open-air fitness center, steam rooms, a Jacuzzi, and a temperature-controlled pool that graces you with vistas of the lake. Prepare for your treatment by savoring a calming tea infused with flavors like lemon, ginger, and cumin seeds. After your session, indulge in a soul-nourishing meal that can be enjoyed al fresco right by the spa pavilion, allowing you to bask in the picturesque views of Lake Pichola.

theleela.com/the-leela-palace-udaipur/experience/wellness

+91 294 670 1203

64 SIX SENSES VANA

Mussoorie Road, 248001 Uttarakhand, India

You'll embark on a modern ashram journey that caters to all your needs.

Six Senses Vana is the first and only dedicated wellness retreat by renowned luxury eco-resort brand Six Senses. What sets it apart is the seamless fusion of Ayurveda, Tibetan medicine, traditional Chinese medicine, and a steadfast commitment to sustainable practices. In fact, Six Senses Vana proudly holds the distinction of being the sole LEED Platinum certified wellness retreat in India. Upon arrival at this expansive 21-acre refuge surrounded by dense sal forest and the Himalayan mountains, you'll undergo a comprehensive wellness screening and consultation. This initial assessment serves as your guiding compass throughout your stay. You can anticipate receiving one private treatment or session per day, complemented by inclusive offerings of nutritious cuisine, refreshing beverages, and comfy kurta pajamas to wear throughout your visit—a testimony to the retreat's "all enter as equals" philosophy.

The retreat's multifaceted programs include yoga, meditation, cooking lessons, functional fitness, insightful talks, soul-stirring music, and more. The array of treatments is equally diverse, ranging from a four-handed Ayurvedic abhyanga massage with fragrant Ayurvedic oils to the transcendent Tibetan Ku Nye massage, which employs warm pods applied along your energy channels while the air resonates with the melodic sounds of Sanskrit mantras. You can also partake in the unique Raag therapy, accompanied by the melodies of a talented flutist. For those seeking contemporary beauty treatments, biohacking compression boots and a luxurious pearl remineralizing body wrap are readily available.

65 THE SPA AT COMO SHAMBHALA ESTATE

Banjar Begawan, Desa Melinggih Kelod,
Payangan, Gianyar, 80571 Bali, Indonesia

In a jungle enclave to the north of Ubud, you'll discover the luxe Como Shambhala Estate. This exceptional resort is known for its impressive spa and tailored wellness programs aimed at immersing guests in physical activities that include personal training sessions, guided adventure challenges, spa treatments and nutritious cuisine. Each day unfolds with a calendar brimming with wellness-focused activities, promising an enriching and transformative stay.

The lavish spa features four open-air pavilions with baths and nine indoor treatment rooms. For those seeking hydrotherapy, there's an outdoor vitality pool, while sauna and steam rooms offer a further chance to relax. Completing the spa's array of facilities is a pool and dedicated fitness and yoga studios and pavilions. The treatment menu includes a hot stone massage, which employs stones sourced from the river below, a traditional Balinese body wrap, acupuncture, and a selection of Ayurvedic treatments. The Javanese Royal LuLur Bath is a standout, drawing from a centuries-old beauty regime once exclusive to the Royal Palaces of Central Java. This pampering experience includes an Indonesian massage, an invigorating body scrub, and an aromatic bath, finishing with a thorough application of lotion.

comohotels.com/bali/
como-shambhala-estate/wellness   +62 361 978 888

66 NIHI SPA SAFARI AT NIHI SUMBA ISLAND

Hoba Wawi, Wanokaka, West Sumba Regency East,
87272 Nusa Tenggara, Indonesia

**TO VISIT
BEFORE YOU DIE
BECAUSE**

You can ride on
horseback to your
spa treatment
in style.

Getting to NIHI Spa Safari from the main NIHI Sumba Island resort, a Leading Hotels of the World member, is an adventure. You can arrive on horseback, in a safari Jeep, or after a vigorous hike, and be prepared to spend a full or half day here. Your spa safari offers complete flexibility. You can begin with a refreshing swim in the sea followed by breakfast cooked on an open fire, or you can settle into one of the treatment huts perched on dramatic cliffs above the sea, where you can indulge in a wide range of treatment options, ranging from Sumbanese massages to stimulating body scrubs and signature facials.

nihi.com/sumba/experiences/
wellness/spa-safari   +62 361 757 149

67 CAPELLA WELLNESS AT CAPELLA UBUD

Jl. Raya Dalem, Banjar Triwangsa, Desa Keliki,
Tegallalang Ubud, Gianyar, 80561 Bali, Indonesia

TO VISIT
BEFORE YOU DIE
BECAUSE

It's a spiritual
awakening like no
other in a verdant
rainforest setting.

Insulate yourself from the outside world at the lush rainforest retreat that is Capella Wellness at Capella Ubud. The spa consists of three luxe treatment tents, a state-of-the-art gym, and a stunning 98-foot outdoor rainforest pool. Here, you can indulge in massages and facials, as well as a collection of Balinese remedies. The spa's treatments are based on lunar energy and celestial rhythm, as well as the significance of water to Balinese Hindus as a purification element. For example, the Full Moon Ritual involves a grounding foot massage, followed by a full body cream exfoliant applied with long soothing strokes, and a massage and facial focusing on facial marma pressure points. A Soul Reborn takes you to the nearby Beji, an ancient spring of rejuvenating holy water, where you will engage in Melukat, a spiritual cleansing ritual guided by a local priest.

capellahotels.com/en/capella-ubud/wellness   +62 361 2091 888

68 AMAN SPA AT AMAN KYOTO

1 Okitayama, Washimine-cho Kita-ku, 603-8458 Kyoto, Japan

TO VISIT
BEFORE YOU DIE
BECAUSE

You'll experience a traditional Japanese onsen in the lap of luxury.

Aman Kyoto, situated near natural mineral springs, embraces Japan's riches in its spa treatments. You can experience traditional indoor and outdoor onsen bathing facilities and treatments incorporating Kyoto green tea, kuromame black beans, sake, cold-pressed camellia oil, and Kyoto silk cocoon. The spa also offers moxibustion, acupuncture, and shiatsu, a specialty of the spa. This intuitive massage technique, based on the principles as acupuncture, aims to restore the flow of qi in the body, and is known to improve muscle tone, stimulate blood and lymph circulation, strengthen immunity, and relieve stress. The property's zen gardens are the site of yoga and mindfulness sessions.

aman.com/resorts/aman-kyoto   +81 75 496 1333

69 THERMAL SPRING SPA AT HOTEL THE MITSUI KYOTO

Nijoaburanokoji-cho 284, Aburano-koji St. Nijo-sagaru, Nakagyo-ku, 604-0051 Kyoto, Japan

TO VISIT
BEFORE YOU DIE
BECAUSE

You can indulge in an authentic Japanese onsen experience, followed by a luxurious pearl facial.

The Thermal Spring Spa at Hotel The Mitsui Kyoto centers around its onsen, drawing healing water from the Kyoto Nijo hot spring located about 3,000 feet directly below the property. While bathing, you'll be surrounded by evocative gray rock walls and large stones accenting the space, and you can enjoy the waterfalls and showers from above. You can also reserve time in the hotel's private onsen suite with Japanese garden views and lounge spaces. The spa offers a variety of facial and body treatments in partnership with Mikimoto Cosmetics that incorporate pearl ingredients, as well as treatments in partnership with Japanese brand Thera and French brand Alaena.

hotelthemitsui.com/en/
kyoto/thermal_springs-spa

+81 75 468 3125

70 HOSHINOYA KARUIZAWA

Nagakura 2148, Karuizawa, Kitasaku District,
389-0111 Nagano, Japan

TO VISIT
BEFORE YOU DIE
BECAUSE

You'll be immersed
in nature in a
meditative manner.

Hoshinoya Karuizawa, the original forest ryokan that initiated the Hoshino Resorts brand, began in 1914 here in Nagano Prefecture, known for its hot springs with therapeutic hot bicarbonate and chloride content. Exclusive to guests at Hoshinoya Karuizawa is the Meditation Bath, a hot spring facility offering both light and dark meditative areas. The open-air public hot spring, Tombo-no-yu, is reserved for hotel guests every morning and is surrounded by the Karuizawa National Wild Bird Sanctuary Forest. The spa at Hoshinoya Karuizawa offers a range of services, including traditional shiatsu, hot stone, and aromatherapy massages. The spa also provides unique therapies that utilize steamed leaf-wrapped pouches filled with rice flour, kneaded with ingredients such as mugwort, dokudami, loquat leaves, or sake lees, depending on the season. The Moonlight Treatment, available only in winter, involves a hot stone massage followed by a moonlit stroll through the Wild Bird Sanctuary.

     hoshinoya.com/karuizawa   +81 50 3134 8091

71

SENSE, A ROSEWOOD SPA AT ROSEWOOD LUANG PRABANG

Ban Nadueay Village, 06000 Luang Prabang, Laos

TO VISIT
BEFORE YOU DIE
BECAUSE

Ancient Lao traditions and native ingredients are fully showcased here.

On a hillside just outside the UNESCO World Heritage Site of the ancient capital of Luang Prabang, is the intimate Rosewood Luang Prabang resort, surrounding a waterfall. Within this serene setting is the tented luxury spa camp, Sense, A Rosewood Spa, featuring three treatment tents. The spa combines Laotian healing remedies with Western techniques, utilizing native herbs, plants, and fruits from the on-site organic garden. The Lost Remedies treatment incorporates Laotian herbal poultices with herbs like crinum lily, camphor tree, Lao coriander, white butterfly bush, and Lao rice to heal pain. Other services include Lao massages with pressure points and stretching, as well as body polishes with locally harvested produce like coconut or passion fruit seed oils. Additionally, the spa offers a five-hour retreat with a Lao Baci ceremony, cleansing water ritual, body scrub, and massage.

rosewoodhotels.com/en/
luang-prabang/wellness/spa   +856 7121 1155

72 SPA & WELLNESS CENTRE AT THE BANJARAN HOTSPRINGS RETREAT

The Banjaran Hotsprings Retreat No. 1, Persiaran Lagun Sunway 3, 31150 Ipoh, Perak Darul Ridzuan, Malaysia

TO VISIT
BEFORE YOU DIE
BECAUSE

You'll absorb the benefits of hot springs and traditional Malay healing in one peaceful location.

The Banjaran Hotsprings Retreat lies within a 22.7-acre valley and is Ipoh, Malaysia's first luxury natural hot springs retreat. The resort boasts natural geothermal hot spring pools and several limestone caves adapted to house a natural sauna and ice bath, plus there is the Meditation Cave and Crystal Cave for reiki sessions and more.

The Spa & Wellness Centre offers a holistic program featuring fitness and consultations, along with treatments rooted in Malay Ramuan wellness philosophy and traditions of indigenous Malay, Chinese, and Indian cultures. The menu includes traditional Chinese medicine, Ayurveda, and Malay Ramaun therapies, such as the 180-minute Hawa Traditional Journey for Women, which combines a traditional Urut massage, hibiscus scrub, body wrap, tangas herbal cleanse, Malay hair cream bath, and Mandi Bunga, a bathing tradition passed down for generations in Malaysia.

sunwayhotels.com/
the-banjaran/wellness/spa   +60 5 210 7777

73

THE SPA
AT RITZ-CARLTON
LANGKAWI

Jalan Pantai Kok PT 313, Kampung Teluk Nibong,
07000 Langkawi, Kedah, Malaysia

TO VISIT
BEFORE YOU DIE
BECAUSE

These Malay *bubu*-inspired treatment pods are one-of-a-kind.

At the Ritz-Carlton Langkawi, you'll discover five open-air, cocoon-shaped pavilions that appear to float on the sea, connected by overwater walkways. These pavilions are designed to invoke Malay *bubus*, intricately woven fish traps used for centuries by local fishermen. Inside these distinctive spa rooms you can choose from a selection of locally inspired healing rituals that have been practiced in the Malay Archipelago for thousands of years. The Mystical Ocean and Earth Ritual combines marine mud and heated volcanic stones, while the Mandi Bunga Inspired Ritual harnesses the power of sacred flowers. The Hammam Pavilion features a marble steam room, ritual pouring seats, and a private scrub chamber with a heated stone bed for traditional exfoliation and foaming. You can pamper yourself further in the thermal areas with a mosaic-clad steam room, a sauna, an invigorating ice fountain, experiential showers, and vitality pools, along with luxurious air loungers that overlook the exquisite landscape.

ritzcarlton.com/en/
hotels/malaysia/langkawi/spa
+60 4 952 4888

74 ANANTARA SPA AT ANANTARA KIHAVAH MALDIVES VILLAS

20215 Kihavah Huravalhi Island, Baa Atoll, Maldives

An Ayurvedic massage in an overwater suite in the Maldives is an unforgettable experience.

At the Anantara Spa at Anantara Kihavah Maldives Villas, you'll be surrounded by the cerulean Indian Ocean on all sides as you're pampered from head to toe in one of six super-luxe overwater treatment suites. Studio Révérence, led by celebrated pedicure-podiatrist Bastien Gonzalez, offers therapeutic manicures and pedicures using French chiropody methods. The resort also houses the region's only Cocoon Medical Spa, providing cutting edge med-spa therapies, including the Cleopatra 24 Carat Gold Collagen Facial, Diamond Microdermabrasion, and non-surgical facelifts. For a more holistic experience, partake in multi-day programs with Balance Wellness that combine exercise, nutrition, and Ayurvedic treatments, guided by qualified naturopaths, nutritional therapists, and wellness experts.

anantara.com/en/kihavah-maldives   +960 664 41 11

75 AREKA AT JOALI BEING

Meedhoo, Maldives

TO VISIT
BEFORE YOU DIE
BECAUSE

It's an entire
island, dedicated
to wellness and
self-discovery.

Dubbed a "wellbeing island," Joali Being offers a personalized journey of self-discovery and renewal amid natural beauty. The island provides expert-led experiential classes, educational workshops, mindful movement opportunities, holistic healing treatments, and farm-to-table cuisine centered around four pillars: mind, microbiome, skin, and energy. Areka, the center of wellness offerings, features 39 treatment rooms and several transformational spaces. These include the Hydrotherapy Hall; a watsu therapy pool; a salt inhalation room; the Discovery Sound Path, a palm-fringed trail leading to a sound therapy oasis with nine instruments to help restore inner balance through harmonizing vibrations and sounds; and a herbology center for treatments and interactive workshops.

76 THE SPA AT THE CHEDI MUSCAT

18th November Street 133, Muscat, Oman

TO VISIT
BEFORE YOU DIE
BECAUSE

This is the ultimate place to experience hijami cupping therapy.

Chedi Muscat, a five-star member of the Leading Hotels of the World, combines beachfront relaxation with proximity to the old city of Muscat. The hotel houses a lavish, Moorish-style spa with eight spacious spa suites, some with private whirlpools for bathing rituals. There's a lofty relaxation area with epic ocean views, plus sauna and steam rooms connected to an expansive fitness center. In addition to Western facials, the spa specializes in a variety of Asian therapies like Balinese, Ayurveda, Thai, and Tibetan wellness philosophies. Also on offer is an array of hijama, or Islamic cupping treatments, which employ a combination of massage techniques, creating negative and positive pressure using suction cups.

ghmhotels.com/en/
muscat/spa-wellness/

+968 24 524400

77 ZULAL WELLNESS RESORT BY CHIVA-SOM

Madīnat ash Shamāl, Al Ruwais, Qatar

This is where you can immerse yourself in traditional Arabic and Islamic medicine.

The largest wellness resort in the Middle East, Zulal Wellness Resort comes from the team behind Thailand's famous Chiva-Som, and focuses on the six pillars of health: fitness, physiotherapy, spa, holistic health, aesthetic beauty, and nutrition. The resort, in a secluded spot at the northernmost tip of Qatar surrounded by the Arabian Sea, offers various wellness retreats guided by the principals of traditional Arabic and Islamic medicine as a holistic path to wellness.

The resort is divided into two sections, one for families and one for adults only, each with expansive wellness facilities including hammams, salt caves, mineral baths, and more. Zulal houses more than 12 types of treatment rooms, and the majority of services are inspired by traditional Arabic and Islamic medicine, ranging from massage al batin (abdominal massage) and al ra (head massage) to hijama (cupping therapy).

78   SPA 1899 DONGINBI

Daechi-dong 1002, Gangnam-gu, 06000 Seoul, South Korea

TO VISIT
BEFORE YOU DIE
BECAUSE

This is the place to uncover the power of red ginseng.

Spa 1899, located in Seoul's Gangnam district, offers a unique experience centered around the power of red ginseng. The spa uses products from Donginbi, a skincare line by Korea Ginseng Corporation, which incorporates aged red ginseng and condensed red ginseng oil. Expert therapists conduct Red Ginseng Energy Circulation Therapies using Donginbi products, creating a ceremonial and specialized spa experience. The spa features a Skin Bar for exploring the Donginbi product line, a Red Ginseng Spa Room for massages and facial treatments, and dedicated areas for foot and head therapy. In the Capsule Zone, concentrated red ginseng is applied to your body before you recline in a heated capsule to release toxins and absorb the red ginseng nutrition. All treatments begin with a refreshing red ginseng tea, and you can choose from a variety of services focusing on the face, body, head, or foot, or opt for a combination.

79   JUNIPER SPA CENTER AT THE WE HOTEL

453-95, 1100-ro, Seogwipo-si, 63551 Jeju, South Korea

The spa harnesses the power of volcanic bedrock water, with expert guidance.

The WE Hotel, tucked at the foot of Mt. Halla on Jeju Island, utilizes the island's natural, mineral-rich volcanic water for its wellness programs. The WE Healing With You program offers various wellness retreats, combining land and water-based scientific therapies.

The hotel features both indoor and outdoor natural volcanic rock pools, Jacuzzis, hinoki saunas, Finnish saunas, and unique water-based equipment, including an ultrasonic water bath using volcanic bedrock water. The surrounding forests are touted for forest bathing walks and meditation. The Juniper Spa Center is the country's first combination medical and massage spa, offering body and facial treatments that target immunity improvement, joint and pain care, and brain function strengthening.

wehotel.co.kr/en/wellness/medical-spa   +82 64 730 1200

80 ANANTARA SPA AT ANANTARA CHIANG MAI

Charoen Prathet Road 123, 123/1,
50100 Tambon Chang Khlan, Chiang Mai, Thailand

This is where traditional Thai medicine comes alive.

Dive into the world of traditional Thai medicine at the Anantara Spa at Anantara Chiang Mai, located along the banks of the Mai Ping River. Traditional Thai medicine is rooted in the Sukhothai period of the 13th century and combines medicinal science and a philosophy of the elements to promote balance and immunity. For a truly memorable experience, book the Pao Ya treatment, which involves a gentle belly massage, followed by the use of herbs set aflame to release heat and promote healing. The spa also offers Lanna treatments, originating from northern Thailand, which draw on the healing properties of fire. In addition to the traditional therapies, the spa boasts modern medical spa technology, such as IV drips with cocktails of vitamins, minerals, antioxidants, and amino acids, along with cell and light therapy. With ten treatment rooms, each equipped with a steam room and terrazzo tub, along with indoor and outdoor relaxation areas, this spa provides a blend of tradition and innovation.

anantara.com/en/chiang-mai/spa   +66 53 253 333

81 CHIVA-SOM

Phet Kasem Road 73/4-6,
77110 Hua Hin, Prachuap Khiri Khan, Thailand

TO VISIT
BEFORE YOU DIE
BECAUSE

This legendary retreat offers results-driven wellness amid beautiful beachfront surroundings.

Chiva-Som, which means "Haven of Life" in Thai, has been a world-renowned wellness sanctuary since 1995. Situated on 6.7 acres of beachfront land in Hua Hin, this exclusive retreat blends Western practices and Eastern philosophies to offer a deeply personal and holistic approach to wellness. All-inclusive, multi-day retreats are based on six wellness modalities: spa, fitness, physiotherapy, holistic health, nutrition, and aesthetic beauty. Guests can participate in daily fitness, wellness, and leisure activities, from meditation and tai chi to Thai boxing and aqua aerobics. The recently refurbished Health & Wellness Centre has a whopping 70 treatment rooms, an outdoor pool, fitness and movement studios, consultation rooms, a bathing pavilion with an exercise pool, Kneipp walk, and wet areas with sauna and steam rooms, whirlpools, and plunge pools. The Niranlada Medi-Spa at Chiva-Som boasts the latest advancements in aesthetic and micro-invasive cosmetic treatments, including Picosure for tattoo and scar removal, and Jetpeel for exfoliation, cleansing, and rehydration.

82   RAKXA

Wat Bang Nam Phueng Alley 28/8 หมู่ 9,
10130 Bang Nam Phueng, Phra Pradaeng District,
Samut Prakan, Thailand

TO VISIT
BEFORE YOU DIE
BECAUSE

This is a modern wellness island retreat just a few minutes away from the chaos of Bangkok.

Amazingly, a true oasis exists just across from bustling Bangkok, on the Chao Phraya River. RAKxa, located on the jungle island of Bang Krachao, is a 21st-century wellness retreat surrounded by nature. The comprehensive program starts with a team of experts who use detailed diagnostics to assess your health. A dedicated advisor will work with you to design a personalized plan to reach your unique health goals. The services offered are extensive and the facilities are top notch. The scientific wellness clinic partners with VitalLife, a renowned partner of Bumrungrad Hospital, to offer modern technologies. The medical gym employs technology and functional medicine to customize holistic exercise routines tailored to your needs. RAKxa Jai, the wellness center, offers a wide range of treatments, from singing bowl healing to flotation sessions and traditional treatments such as navarakizhi, which uses medicinal red rice, milk, and herbs (tied in a cloth) for massages.

83 CAĞALOĞLU HAMMAM

Alemdar, Prof. Kazım İsmail Gürkan Cd. No:24,
34110 Fatih/İstanbul, Türkiye

TO VISIT
BEFORE YOU DIE
BECAUSE

This historic hammam is as beautiful as it is authentic.

Türkiye has a long history of hammams, and the Cağaloğlu Hammam was first constructed in 1741 as a double men's and women's public bath, making it the last bath to be built during the Ottoman Empire. The hammam features impressive architecture, with soaring gray and white marble domes that allow streaming light to create a tranquil ambience. The interior has thick columns and arches adorned with wood accents and tasseled lanterns. The separate men's and women's sides are equally captivating. Guests can choose from a selection of six traditional hammam treatments, ranging from the 45-minute basic sauna-style rest and scrub with the exfoliating kese glove to a two-hour-plus extravaganza with two therapists, including a clay mask and aromatherapy massage in addition to the basic service.

84   HÜRREM SULTAN HAMMAM

Cankurtaran, Ayasofya Meydanı No:2,
34122 Fatih/İstanbul, Türkiye

TO VISIT
BEFORE YOU DIE
BECAUSE

This is the place to experience authentic Turkish rituals in a hammam built for a sultana.

A historic Istanbul hammam, the Hürrem Sultan Hammam was built in 1556 by Mimar Sinan at the request of Hurrem Sultan (Roxelana), the wife of Sultan Suleiman the Magnificent. The hammam, which was operational until 1910, underwent a meticulous restoration in 2008. During the restoration, 14,000 square feet of marmara marble was used, preserving much of the original structure. The hammam consists of three sections: the cold area with changing rooms; the warm area, where scrubbing takes place; and the hot area featuring a large marble navel stone that lies under the hammam's lofty dome. The hot room is where you'll enjoy a bubble wash and massage after your scrub. The hammam offers four traditional hammam rituals and four different massage therapies.

hurremsultanhamami.com   +90 212 517 3535

85　SIX SENSES SPA AT SIX SENSES KAPLANKAYA

Bozbük Mahallesi Merkez Sokak No: 198,
Milas, Muğla, 48200, Türkiye

The expansive Six Senses Spa, one of the largest in the world at 107,640 square feet, provides an integrative approach to wellness with core programs such as holistic anti-aging, weight-loss clinics, and sleep health lasting from three to 14 days. The spa is at the heart of Six Senses Kaplankaya, across the bay from Bodrum and surrounded by undulating hills dotted with evergreens, ancient olive trees, and cypresses. The spa sports a massive hydrotherapy area where you can indulge in various saunas, steam rooms, hammams, hydrotherapy pools, experiential showers, an igloo, and a salt room. At the Alchemy Bar, guests can blend locally sourced ingredients to create a bespoke scrub for their treatment. The extensive treatment menu encompasses everything from Western massages and facials to Turkish hammam rituals, watsu sessions, and Ayurvedic therapies. The locally inspired Rejuvenating Herbal Quartz Poultice Journey draws from the ancient tradition of earthing, to help ground the body. The journey starts with creating herbal poultices, which are then used during a dry massage carried out on a heated and tilted quartz bed, followed by a head massage while reclining on a zero-gravity bed.

sixsenses.com/en/
resorts/kaplankaya/wellness-spa　　　　+90 252 511 0030

86 ANANTARA SPA AT QASR AL SARAB BY ANANTARA

Qasr Al Sarab Road 1, Abu Dhabi, United Arab Emirates

TO VISIT
BEFORE YOU DIE
BECAUSE

Surrounded by sand, you'll find true tranquility.

Located 90 minutes from Abu Dhabi in the world's largest sand desert, the Empty Quarter, you'll discover the oasis-like Qasr Al Sarab by Anantara. Inside the castle-like structure is the Anantara Spa, featuring five luxurious treatment suites for individuals and couples, an authentic Moroccan hammam, two steam rooms, an ice room, a sauna, private yoga rooms, a dedicated medical wellness center for IV therapies, an outdoor Thai sala, and a relaxation area with epic views of the red sand dunes that stretch across the Empty Quarter. Treat yourself to a range of massages, body therapies, and facials, or book a signature treatment that combines several services, such as the Arabian Desert Rose Ritual, a 240-minute experience that includes a floral foot ritual, body scrub, rhassoul body mask, rose milk bath, rose body massage, and Biologique Recherche facial using rose-themed elements for the ultimate desert rejuvenation.

anantara.com/en/
qasr-al-sarab-abu-dhabi/spa

+971 2 886 2088

87 AWAKEN AT ATLANTIS THE ROYAL

Crescent Road, Dubai, United Arab Emirates

TO VISIT
BEFORE YOU DIE
BECAUSE

If you seek over-the-top pampering in one of the finest spas in the world, this is your destination.

Located in the striking Atlantis The Royal building in Dubai, AWAKEN aims to awaken the elements of nature in each guest: body (earth), mind (fire), emotion (water) and spirit (air). Spanning 54,303 square feet of indoor and outdoor facilities, the spa features the Hammam Sensorium with six-rooms and an Elements Circuit inspired by the four elements. The circuit includes a charcoal sauna and tepidarium for fire, halotherapy salt rooms and meditation gardens for earth, a hydrotherapy pool and alchemy shower for water, and an aromatherapy steam room and air loungers for air. For treatments, you'll be ensconced in one of the 15 therapy suites equipped with fireplaces, dressing areas, and private showers. For a localized experience, try the Desert Sand & Date Sugar Infusion, an exfoliation treatment with oud-infused Dubai desert sand and date sugar, followed by a Khaliji pink clay wrap and date shea butter application. For the ultimate luxury, choose the Golden Hour, a massage that uses hot volcanic stones layered in precious metals and 24-karat gold-infused aromatic oil.

atlantis.com/atlantis-the-royal/
awaken-wellness

+971 4 426 2131

88 THE SPA AT EMIRATES PALACE MANDARIN ORIENTAL ABU DHABI

West Corniche Road, Al Ras Al Akhdar,
Abu Dhabi, United Arab Emirates

TO VISIT
BEFORE YOU DIE
BECAUSE

You'll have a palatial experience.

Hidden behind impressive, ornately carved walls, the Spa at Emirates Palace Mandarin Oriental Abu Dhabi offers a stunning and mystical desert ambience. Decorated with dim lanterns, bubbling water features, colorful wall mosaics, and perfumed with scents of neroli and orange blossom, this spa blends Moroccan, indigenous Arabian therapies, and Eastern wellness practices with contemporary spa and beauty treatments.

The vast treatment menu includes four rituals in a gorgeous hammam, five bathing experiences, eight facials, five massages, and numerous other specialized experiences. In the opulent Essence of Abu Dhabi treatment, you'll experience the power of citrine crystals and CBD through a body scrub, followed by a gold dust massage and the application of gold facial ampoules, giving your skin a radiant glow.

89

JSPA
AT SPA-HOTEL JAGDHOF

Scheibe 44, 6167 Neustift, Stubai Valley, Tyrol, Austria

TO VISIT
BEFORE YOU DIE
BECAUSE

The Austrian
Alps are an idyllic
backdrop for
a mountain
spa retreat.

Nestled in the stunning Stubai Valley in Tyrol, the Relais & Châteaux member Spa-Hotel Jagdhof offers a captivating alpine spa retreat. The jSpa spans 32,000 square feet and houses 12 treatment rooms, 20 saunas, Kneipp baths, steam rooms, salt rooms, and indoor and outdoor pools. Many of the spa's treatments are alpine-inspired, such as the Mountain Pine Massage, which commences with a scrub of honey and Austrian stone pine, followed by a massage with aromatic stone pine oil. Additionally, there is a robust menu of balneology-focused services. The spa's log-cabin-inspired spa chalet, adorned with original wildlife artwork by Hubert Weidinger, is built from reclaimed Tyrolean wood and features an array of loungers and hammocks, both indoors and outdoors, some positioned beside crackling fireplaces, and is equipped with a well-stocked tea bar. For an even more indulgent experience, you can reserve the private spa suite, where you can enjoy your very own pine Finnish sauna, an aromatherapy shower, an infinity duo pool complete with color light therapy, hammock loungers for two offering views of the Stubai Glacier, a cozy bed by the fireplace, and even a Champagne minibar. Prost!

hotel-jagdhof.at/en/wellness-hotel   +43 5226 2666

90 THE SPA AT ROGNER BAD BLUMAU

Bad Blumau 100, 8283 Bad Blumau, Austria

TO VISIT
BEFORE YOU DIE
BECAUSE

You can relax in a whimsical environment surrounded by the beauty of nature.

This extraordinary village-like hotel, tucked away in the Austrian Alps, was designed by the renowned Austrian artist Friedensreich Hundertwasser, celebrated for his imaginative and colorful architectural creations and artwork. Rogner Bad Blumau has an array of buildings, characterized by patchwork designs and vibrant undulating forms, arranged like a charming city with distinct districts. At the heart of it all is the ring-shaped spa from which the accommodation, pools, and restaurant areas radiate out into the beautiful open landscape. The hotel and spa draw water from the underground geothermal Vulkania spring, providing sustainable power for the entire resort and supplying healing waters for the spa. The spa itself comprises two bathing lakes and an Olympic-size swimming pool, constantly replenished with fresh water from the Vulkania spring. It also features a selection of thermal baths with varying temperatures, and more than ten distinct saunas and steam rooms. Within the spa, a rich menu of treatments awaits, offering more than a dozen massages, about ten different facials, and a wide range of body treatments and scrubs, including Ayurveda and hammam-inspired options.

91

THE SPA
AT STANGLWIRT

Kaiserweg 1, 6353 Going am Wilden Kaiser, Austria

TO VISIT
BEFORE YOU DIE
BECAUSE

Here is where
to turn the
Austrian Alps
into your wellness
playground.

Stanglwirt has been a family establishment since 1722, offering an organic farm and a five-star Tyrolean wellness resort at the base of the breathtaking Wilder Kaiser mountain range. Covering a sprawling 130,000 square feet, the large spa boasts a charming outdoor rock pool and whirlpool, an organic pine-clad sauna (among five saunas and three steam baths), a salt-water pool, a waterfall grotto, and relaxation areas with uninterrupted mountain views.

The highly trained spa staff pampers guests with an array of relaxing and effective treatments, such as classic massages and facials, Ayurvedic body treatments, and Rolfing, an integrated system of manual body work developed in 1950 by Dr. Ida Rolf to relieve pain and improve posture. The spa also provides an extensive fitness program, with classes ranging from yoga, Pilates, and aqua aerobics to Nordic walking, tennis, golf, mountain biking, hiking, rock climbing, horseback riding, and skiing in winter.

stanglwirt.com/
en/wellnesshotel/spa-services.html   +43 5358 2000

92   **ENERGIA ECO-SPA**

Vihi, 71402 Viljandi County, Estonia

TO VISIT
BEFORE YOU DIE
BECAUSE

This spa allows you to explore traditional Estonian remedies with onsite medicinal herb cultivation.

Situated on the banks of the Navesti River in southwestern Estonia, about an hour-and-a-half from Tallinn, the Energia Eco-Spa immerses you into a natural lifestyle rooted in the traditional wisdom of past generations. All wellness therapies at the spa are based on the centuries-old Estonian tradition of using medicinal plants. The Energia farm serves as the largest medicinal plant growing center in the country, cultivating organic chamomile, calendula, St. John's wort, mint, and other plants, which are grown and processed here for use in traditional herbal treatment methods. The spa has two saunas, where you can request birch, juniper, oak, or linden branches to enhance your banya experience, a cold-water tub, and a whirlpool infused with herbal aromas. You can also take a bracing dip in the Navesti River or treat yourself to a comprehensive experience that incorporates freshly harvested herbs along with clay, peat, and natural plant oils delivered through baths, wraps, and massages. Post-treatment, explore the three herbal study and health trails—the energy trail, relaxing trail, and stress relief trail—where you can admire the beauty of herbs, savor their aroma, and learn how to use them medicinally.

visitestonia.com/en/energy-eco-spa   +372 510 6193

93 THE SPA AT LES SOURCES DE CAUDALIE

Chemin de Smith Haut Lafitte,
33650 Bordeaux-Martillac, France

TO VISIT
BEFORE YOU DIE
BECAUSE

This is the ultimate destination for vinotherapy treatments.

One of the world's premier vinotherapy spas, the spa at Les Sources de Caudalie in Bordeaux pioneered the use of a therapeutic combination of hot spring water, vine, and grape extracts for its trademark Vinothérapie. Located amidst the vines of the Château Smith Haut Lafitte, Grand Cru Classé de Graves, the family-owned Les Sources de Caudalie embraces the concept of the French Paradox, recognizing the preventative qualities of red wine due to its numerous antioxidants. All Les Sources de Caudalie treatments feature the renowned Caudalie cosmetics, created onsite and based on innovative uses of active polyphenol components found in grape pips. The barn-style spa features 20 treatment rooms, an indoor greenhouse pool adorned with artwork by Mathilde de L'Ecotais, a thermal bathing area with a Jacuzzi and hammam, and a relaxation room offering views of the surrounding vineyards. Indulge in exclusive therapies such as the Crushed Cabernet Scrub, Honey and Wine Wrap, Barrel Bath, and Winemaker's Massage, or splurge on comprehensive curative wellness programs that span several days.

sources-caudalie.com/
en/spa-caudalie-bordeaux   +33 5 5783 8383

94 LOISEAU DES SENS SPA AT LE RELAIS BERNARD LOISEAU

Avenue Bernard Loiseau 2, 21210 Saulieu, France

You'll inhale Burgundy's beauty while treating yourself to a cutting-edge hydrotherapy experience.

Sct within the Morvan Regional National Park in Burgundy, Le Relais Bernard Loiseau, a member of Relais & Châteaux, is a tranquil retreat surrounded by forests. Villa Loiseau des Sens, the spa building that opened in 2017, is built from Douglas fir and Morvan oak, blending harmoniously with the historic relais buildings, gardens, and forests. The spa, occupying more than 16,000 square feet, features a multisensory pool offering various hydrotherapies, including a bubbling bench, aqua bikes, jetted massage cubicles, and a hydronox bench for a "zero gravity" experience. A second area, dubbed the Pleasure Universe, houses a sauna, steam rooms, experiential showers, an ice fountain, waterfall bucket, and a sea air cabin. With ten treatment rooms and a private VIP suite on the top floor offering mountain views, you can indulge in services such as Olivier Claire or Clé des Champs facials, body scrubs, and the Renaissance Signature Treatment Massage, complete with a footbath, muscular massage, and breathing exercises.

bernard-loiseau.com/
en/bernardloiseau-spa.html

+33 3 8090 5353

95

THE SPA
AT MANDARIN
ORIENTAL PARIS

Rue Saint-Honoré 251, 75001 Paris, France

TO VISIT
BEFORE YOU DIE
BECAUSE

This is a peaceful, traditional Chinese medicine temple amid the bustling heart of Paris.

As you step through the enormous white sphere at the entrance to the spa at Mandarin Oriental Paris, and the gong sounds, tranquility washes over you. From there, your therapist will assist you in assessing the balance of your yin and yang, and your alignment with one of the five elements. This assessment is based on a traditional Chinese medicine questionnaire that is used at all Mandarin Oriental spas.

With seven spacious treatment rooms, each with their own private bathroom, shower, and changing area, there's no need to share a locker room. The elegant design of each room incorporates the butterfly motif, a central theme throughout the hotel. The 80-minute signature massage, utilizing an essential oil blend that corresponds to your element, will transport you to a state of bliss. After your treatment your therapist will provide guidance on other aspects of your associated element, including daily stretches and actions to incorporate into your routine. The spa also features a large indoor pool, Jacuzzi, and sauna.

mandarinoriental.com/
en/paris/place-vendome/spa
+33 1 7098 7335

96 SPA NOLINSKI BY LA COLLINE AT NOLINKSI PARIS

Avenue de l'Opéra 16, 75001 Paris, France

TO VISIT
BEFORE YOU DIE
BECAUSE

It's a favorite of models during fashion week, making it a worthy wellness destination.

Tucked away beneath the buzzing Avenue de l'Opéra in Paris, the chic spa at Nolinski Paris is a favorite among the fashion-forward. The spa's ambience is crafted with dark tones and subtle gold and star-studded ceilings in the treatment rooms, creating a peaceful space for top-notch therapies. The treatments feature products from Swiss cult favorite La Colline that focus on anti-aging, inspired by the Swiss Alps. Combat jet lag and refresh tired skin with the Gentle Treatment, which includes a full body scrub using a salt or sugar-based scrub, followed by a relaxing steamy shower in your treatment room. Subsequently, you'll be pampered with a massage using the essential oil of your choice, ensuring your muscles melt into submission. Post-treatment, sip a hot tea by the black and gold indoor pool with a mirrored ceiling—one of the most deluxe in Paris. Don't forget to make use of the dry sauna and steam room.

97 SPA LE BRISTOL BY LA PRAIRIE AT LE BRISTOL

Rue du Faubourg Saint-Honoré 112, 75008 Paris, France

It's a chance to indulge in the finest skin products in one of the world's finest hotel spas.

Upon entering the lobby of the iconic Le Bristol hotel in Paris, you are instantly immersed in Old World opulence. Heading to the spa, things take a more modern turn, but remain exceptionally stylish. There are seven treatment rooms, including a duo room with a glass shower and jetted hot tub, ideal for parents who can access the adjacent kids' club specifically available to spa guests. Swiss cosmetics brand La Prairie supplies most of the facial products, while a new collaboration with Tata Harper introduces an organic option with its own treatment room, reminiscent of a Parisian apartment (pictured above). The spa's technologically advanced HydraFacial machine can be added on to any facial to exfoliate, remove impurities, and hydrate with potent antioxidants. The Russian Room features a hammam where you can undergo a traditional banya-style treatment, complete with contrast therapy and birch branch brushing. Following your treatment, savor ginger tea and dried fruit before heading to the sixth floor to enjoy the hotel's famous ship-inspired indoor pool, where you'll feel like you're aboard the world's most luxurious yacht, designed by the craftsman who built the yachts of Stavros Niarchos and Aristotle Onassis.

oetkercollection.com/
hotels/le-bristol-paris/spa-wellness   +33 1 5343 4300

98 GUERLAIN SPA AT RELAIS CHRISTINE

Rue Christine 3, 75006 Paris, France

TO VISIT
BEFORE YOU DIE
BECAUSE

There is no better place to escape to than a magnificent underground wellness cave in Paris.

The boutique hotel Relais Christine, hidden away on a quiet side street in the Left Bank's Latin Quarter, is a peaceful haven from frenzied Paris. In the Relais & Châteaux hotel's basement, which was originally an abbey, you'll discover the even more secluded Guerlain Spa. The spa has preserved the abbey's original cave-like stone walls, well, and fireplace, adding an elegant touch with vibrant flowers and Guerlain glass perfume bottles. Treatment rooms feature exquisite murals on one wall and a crystal bee (the Guerlain logo) placed under the massage bed for you to admire when lying face down. The two-hour signature treatment combines a facial and a massage, allowing you to choose your own Guerlain scented oil, transporting you to a state of bliss. Spa amenities include a fitness center in another cave-like space, an octagon shaped hot tub in a private alcove, and a sauna and steam room.

99   FRIEDRICHSBAD

Römerpl. 1, 76530 Baden-Baden, Germany

TO VISIT
BEFORE YOU DIE
BECAUSE

This is a historic, landmark bathhouse in one of Europe's most famous spa towns.

In the fabled city of Baden-Baden, known for its curative mineral-rich thermal waters that flow from beneath the Florentinerberg hillside, stands the landmark Friedrichsbad bathhouse. This architectural gem, which opened in 1877 in a beautiful Renaissance-style building, remains as captivating today as it was in its heyday, hailed as the most modern bathhouse in Europe at the time. With intricate shower fittings, hand-painted majolica tiles, and the astonishing domed bath, every bathing experience here is memorable. To truly appreciate it, follow the 17 different stations that alternate between mineral showers of varying temperatures, soap and brushing massages, steam baths, and relaxation areas. The waters are sourced from 12 distinct sodium chloride-bearing artesian springs, some dating back 12,000 to 17,000 years. You can also tour the remains of a Roman-era bath before or after your time at this relatively modern spa.

carasana.de/en/friedrichsbad0   +49 7221 275 920

100 LANSERHOF SYLT

Am Lanserhof 1-8, 25992 List, Germany

You'll bask in a medically based wellness transformation in one of the world's most exclusive destinations.

Lanserhof Sylt is the fusion of two extraordinary elements: the Lanserhof Group, renowned for more than 30 years of innovative medicine, and the windswept island of Sylt, often called the playground for Germany's elite. When Lanserhof Sylt opened in 2022, it became the newest and most spectacular addition to the trio of Lanserhof medical spas in Germany and Austria, all adhering to the Lanserhof Cure. This cure is founded on the principles of Austrian holistic physician Franz Xaver Mayr, who specialized in gastrointestinal health. Over the last three decades, it has evolved into a comprehensive wellness approach. During your minimum seven-night stay at Lanserhof Sylt, you will undergo a personalized wellness program encompassing medical and hormonal analysis, reflexology, massages, detox programs, IV infusions, and nutritional guidance. The resort's minimalist design, featuring steeply pitched thatched roofs and glass walls with sweeping sea views, echoes the local architectural style. The massive 215,000-square-foot space includes modern treatment rooms, consultation rooms, exercise facilities, saunas, steam baths, relaxation areas, and an indoor-outdoor saltwater pool with a counter-current system.

lanserhof.com/en/lanserhof-sylt   +49 4651 995 9570

101 THE SPA AT SCHLOSS ELMAU

In Elmau 2, 82493 Elmau, Germany

With six different spa areas, you're certain to find one that suits your preferences.

The German Alps' pristine Elmau Valley is the setting for the Schloss Elmau resort, a member of the Leading Hotels of the World with three adult and three family spas. These encompass various outdoor infinity lap pools sustainably heated by wood chips year-round, indoor lap pools, Japanese onsen pools, a diverse range of steam baths and saunas, and the largest hammam west of Istanbul. The impressive facility houses three large dome rooms with hot stones and water tubs, four treatment rooms, two steam baths, and a tea lounge. The extensive menu of massages offers a global array, including Hawaiian Lomi Lomi, Thai massage, and Chinese tui na. In addition to numerous hammam treatments and facials, the spa offers a variety of targeted wellness retreats, including Strengthen Your Back, Get Back Into Shape, and Reset & Energize. It also hosts yoga and tai chi retreats that integrate Western and traditional Chinese medicines.

102   EUPHORIA RETREAT

Mystras, 231 00 Sparta, Greece

TO VISIT
BEFORE YOU DIE
BECAUSE

You can discover your inner Greek Spartan while experiencing the synergy of Greek and Chinese healing philosophies.

In the mythical and fertile Peloponnese region at the base of Mount Taygetus lies the holistic wellness Euphoria Retreat, inspired by both Greek and Chinese healing philosophies. Its striking architecture draws on the byzantine architecture of the nearby Mystras, a UNESCO World Heritage Site. Designed to harmonize the five elements and the five senses, Euphoria Retreat's goal is not only total transformation, but also to educate you on how to apply holistic wellness practices to your daily life. At the heart of the resort lies a large spherical pool, while the massive spa complex includes a tepidarium, a byzantine hammam, an infrared and laconium Finnish sauna, a salt cave, a watsu pool, and yoga and fitness studios. Treatments include energy healing, cosmetic facials, massages, and specialized treatments like acupuncture and osteopathy. The resort also has several multi-day retreats, such as the Spartan Spirit of Adventure, allowing you to become a real-world warrior.

103 CANAVES OIA SUITES

Main Street, 847 02 Oía, Santorini, Greece

Cool and dark cave-style rooms provide respite from the sweltering Santorini sun.

The Cycladic island of Santorini is teeming with tourists in summer, but at the luxurious Canaves hotel overlooking the breathtaking caldera, the subterranean spa provides an escape from both the crowds and the sun. It's naturally cool environment is due to its location inside an original, centuries-old wine cave. A unique hammam is tucked away in this charming cave, boasting delicate tiles and comfortable steam chairs. Two all-white treatment rooms, embodying the classic Santorini architectural style, provide top-quality treatments, such as the two-hour-and-15-minute combination massage and Valmont facial, leaving your skin glowing from the inside out.

canaves.com/spa-santorini   +30 22860 71453

104 EVEXIA SPA AT ANDRONIS ARCADIA

847 02, Oia, Santorini, Greece

TO VISIT
BEFORE YOU DIE
BECAUSE

Boho-natural décor
and the scenic
surroundings are
an ideal backdrop
for rejuvenation.

Away from the crowds at the caldera in Oia, you'll find the Evexia Spa at Andronis Arcadia, a member of L.V.X. Preferred Hotels & Resorts, offering first-class facilities and skilled therapists. The spa features a dual hot and cold stone-bottomed Kneipp walk, a steam room, a sauna, a gym and a yoga studio. You can spend an entire day here, surrounded by an open-air relaxation area adorned with lush plants, comfy loungers, and hammocks. The spa comprises five treatment rooms and two outdoor treatment pavilions, where you can indulge in signature treatments like Chakra Healing, which begins with an invigorating full-body scrub, followed by a deep-tissue full body, face, and scalp massage, and culminates with shirodhara, an Ayurvedic technique in which warm oil is poured over your third eye. After your treatment, your therapist will offer a delicious and reviving tea to help your return to the real world.

andronis.com/hotels/
andronis-arcadia/explore/evexia-spa   +30 2286 027392

105 ANDRONIS CONCEPT WELLNESS RESORT

Epar.Od. Firon-Ias, 847 00 Thira, Santorini, Greece

TO VISIT
BEFORE YOU DIE
BECAUSE

It's a boutique wellness retreat on a popular Greek island with a waterfall cave pool.

The spa is at the heart of the boutique Andronis Concept Wellness Retreat, where you'll also find healthy meal options, a full roster of fitness classes, and various mindfulness workshops at the resort. Inside the spa, a peaceful, cave-like environment designed with neutral colors and stones invites total calm. You can chose from three oil blends—Energy, Rest & Calm, and Balance—crafted from plants cultivated on an organic farm in Crete. Treatments include the two-hour Balance Ritual, which combines a foot ritual, myofascial massage, a head and scalp release, and a tea ritual. You can enhance any treatment with a bathing ritual or detoxifying clay body mask. Afterwards, unwind in the cave pool with its trickling waterfall and a separate infinity pool for added luxury.

106 LAVA SPA AT MAGMA RESORT SANTORINI, THE UNBOUND COLLECTION BY HYATT

84700 Vourvoulos, Santorini, Greece

TO VISIT BEFORE YOU DIE BECAUSE

With its size and attention to detail, it's one of Santorini's largest and most remarkable spas.

Located just outside Fira, Magma Resort Santorini has a volcanic theme and is surrounded by vineyards. Its Lava Spa is among the largest on the island and boasts an indoor heated pool, a spacious hammam with a Vichy shower table, and a sizeable dry sauna. Thoughtful details include a carefully arranged platter with beautiful shells on the floor below the massage table, offering a delightful sight as you lie face down. The spa's treatments make the most of the island's natural resources, like the Aegean Blue, utilizing five different types of algae in an innovative slimming treatment that activates the energy mechanism of fat cells, promoting a revitalized sense of wellbeing. Meanwhile, the Magma massage uses seashells to transport natural calcium ions to the skin, easing muscle tension, calming the nervous system, and enhancing blood circulation. Post-treatment, sip on Greek mountain tea by the pool.

107 ELIOS SPA AT VEDEMA, A LUXURY COLLECTION RESORT

847 00 Megalochori, Santorini, Greece

TO VISIT
BEFORE YOU DIE
BECAUSE

You'll have an
experience inspired
by the unique
surroundings of
an ancient wine-
making village.

In the traditional Greek village of Megalochori, surrounded by vineyards, lies the boutique hotel Vedema, a Luxury Collection Resort. Seamlessly integrated into the village, the hotel surrounds a 400-year-old stone wine cave, which now houses the hotel's restaurant and a wine cellar with a tasting room. Adjacent to this, in a 100-year-old wine cave, is the petite sanctuary of Elios Spa.

Exemplifying the classic Cycladic style with its all-white décor, the spa is adorned with carefully chosen ceramics and plants. The treatments at Elios Spa showcase Greek brands Korres and Ariadne Athens, and utilize ingredients like crocus, white pine, and Santorini grapes. A standout experience is the Wine Harvest Body Ritual, which involves the application of a rich body mask made from organic honey and wine extracts, followed by a massage with botanical oil and warm pouches filled with Greek herbs, and culminating in the application of a refreshing gel containing red grapes.

108   THE SPA AT CALILO

Papas Beach, 840 01 Ios, Greece

This magical, colorful setting is truly one-of-a-kind in the spa world.

On the Cycladic island of Ios, a rocky, mountainous landscape reveals winding roads and mostly sleepy villages. However, upon arriving at Papas Beach and the fantastical world of Calilo, you are greeted by an explosion of color and love. Brimming with the vibrant artwork of owner Angelos Michalopoulos and inspired by his philosophy of "Create a Life You Can Fall in Love With," the spa resides in a newly built structure complete with a fitness center, an outdoor pool, and a variety of Michalopoulos' colorful marble mosaics. The spa has three open-air treatment rooms that are like nothing you've seen before—massage tables seem to float above water, while massive tree branches adorned with leaves and flowers span the open-plan room. Michalopoulos' signature ceiling cut-outs in hearts and spirals project their illuminated form on the floor and water. Despite the flamboyant atmosphere, the therapists' expertise shines through.

calilo.com/en/category/
spa-wellness-experiences   +30 2286 440740

109 THE SPA AT FOUR SEASONS ASTIR PALACE HOTEL ATHENS

Apollonos 40, 166 71 Vouliagmeni, Greece

TO VISIT
BEFORE YOU DIE
BECAUSE

The white marble of the spa rooms against the deep blue of the Aegean Sea is simply stunning.

Upon entering this luxurious oceanfront spa in the Athens Riviera, you'll find yourself enveloped by pristine white marble and clean, elegant lines. A departure from the norm where spas are often tucked away in basements, this one offers magnificent panoramic views of the dazzling Aegean Sea from its relaxation and treatment rooms. Notably, each of the ten treatment rooms have a balcony overlooking the ocean, where a grounding hand massage ritual takes place before any spa service. Treatments range from a body scrub using local lavender and olive oil to a four-handed massage to combat jet lag, and there are even spa treatments designed for children to enjoy alongside their parents in a family spa suite. Following your treatment, unwind in the indoor pool and hydrotherapy zone, or simply indulge in the cozy lounge rooms, where there's hand-prepared herbal teas, healthy snacks, and refreshing spa water.

fourseasons.com/athens/spa   +30 21 0890 1000

110 ROYAL SPA AT CORINTHIA BUDAPEST

Erzsébet körút 43-49, 1073 Budapest, Hungary

TO VISIT
BEFORE YOU DIE
BECAUSE

This elegant landmark spa boasts a rich history with incredibly healing mineral waters.

Housed in an elegant art deco edifice, the Royal Spa has a storied history, originating in 1888 as a haven where city residents sought the benefits of healing mineral waters. Just a few years later in 1896, the Grand Hotel Royal was built around the spa, firmly establishing it as a premier attraction. However, after enduring decades of closure following World War II, the hotel and spa were meticulously restored to their original splendor in the 2000s, emerging as Corinthia Budapest. Located in the heart of the city, renowned for its healing mineral waters, the spa's facilities include an oversized indoor mineral pool with grand columns, Niagara bathtubs, mud and seaweed baths, Jacuzzis, saunas, steam rooms, and six treatment rooms. Treatments use Espa products for restorative facials, calming massages, and invigorating body scrubs.

corinthia.com/budapest/royal-spa   +36 1 479 4650

111   SZÉCHENYI BATHS

Allatkerti körút 9-11, 1146 Budapest, District XIV, Hungary

TO VISIT
BEFORE YOU DIE
BECAUSE

This is the grandest place to soak in the Spa capital of the world.

The capital city of Budapest has more hot springs than any other capital city worldwide, with temperatures ranging from warm to boiling hot. The Turks built much of the spa infrastructure in the 1500s, and in the 19th century many of the city's beautiful bathhouses were built. Today, Budapest, often referred to as the Spa capital of the world, is home to 123 baths, including the massive Széchenyi Baths. The Neo-Baroque and Neo-Renaissance bath palace in City Park is one of Europe's largest bath complexes, attracting 1.8 million visitors annually. Renowned for its striking blue-tiled architecture and the legendary chess games played while soaking in the outdoor pool, the spa has 18 medicinal indoor and outdoor water pools, including the outdoor adventure pool, a hot tub, a swimming pool, a drift pool, and even beer baths.

112 KRAUMA GEOTHERMAL BATHS

Deildartunguhver, 320 Reykholt, Iceland

You can soak in a thermal hot spring under the wavering Northern Lights.

Set in the remote Icelandic countryside, surrounded by picture-perfect glaciers and mountains, the Krauma Geothermal Baths offer a unique adventure. Due to its remote location far away from city lights, visitors have an excellent chance of witnessing the Northern Lights while soaking in the thermal waters. Nevertheless, even without the Northern Lights, a soak in Krauma's mineral-rich waters, sourced from Deildartunguhver, Europe's most powerful hot spring, is a rewarding experience. Krauma features five baths of varying temperatures, ranging from 39°C (102°F) to 36°C (97°F), complemented by a cold tub for cooling down. The spacious spa area also has a steam room, a relaxation room, and an onsite restaurant.

113   BJÓRBÖÐIN

Ægisgata 31, 621 Dalvík, Iceland

TO VISIT
BEFORE YOU DIE
BECAUSE

**You can bathe
in beer.**

Ever dreamed of bathing in beer? Well, now you can. Also known as the Beer Spa, Bjórböðin is an only-in-Iceland experience. The spa features seven bathtubs, each accommodating two people. During your 25-minute-soak in the tub, you'll be immersed in a mixture of young beer, water, hops, and yeast. The beer's low pH helps tighten and soften your hair follicles, while the hops, rich in antioxidants and alpha acids, are believed to have a relaxing effect on tired muscles. Additionally, you can enjoy the two large cedarwood hot tubs and an outdoor sauna with breathtaking views of Hrísey island, mountains, and Porvalds Valley. And don't forget to savor a locally brewed Kaldi beer at the bar. Skål!

114   SKY LAGOON

Vesturvör 44-48, 200 Kópavogur, Iceland

**TO VISIT
BEFORE YOU DIE
BECAUSE**

Iceland's
geothermal lagoons
are legendary, and
this one offers
a more secluded
experience.

One of Iceland's newest thermal baths, the intimate Sky Lagoon opened in 2021 in Kársnes Harbour, Kópavogur, a mere 15-minute drive from Reykjavik's center on a secluded peninsula overlooking the Atlantic Ocean. The geothermal lagoon boasts a dramatic oceanside infinity edge, showcasing expansive Atlantic Ocean views. Beyond the lagoon, you can immerse yourself in a restorative seven-step experience, inspired by Icelandic bathing traditions, known as the Ritual. This sequence includes a warm lagoon swim, followed by a cold plunge, relaxation in a traditional Icelandic turf house, time in the sauna, an energizing cold mist, exfoliation with a sea salt body scrub, a steam room session, and a final refreshing shower.

115 ELEMENTS TRAIL SPA AT FINN LOUGH

Letter Road 33, BT93 2BB, Aghnablaney, Enniskillen,
County Fermanagh, Northern Ireland, United Kingdom

TO VISIT
BEFORE YOU DIE
BECAUSE

This is your own
personal spa
nature trail.

Seeking an escape to nature? Look no further. Set in Northern Ireland, Finn Lough takes its cues from nature, incorporating thoughtful design and stylish spaces to create a lakeside haven. Besides morning yoga inside a transparent bubble on Lough Erne, the Elements Trail Spa offers a private, self-guided path through nature that leads you through a series of five forest treatment rooms. The Epsom salt float bath delivers a weightless sensation that is deeply relaxing. The Finnish sauna combines the benefits of heat with stunning natural scenery. If you're up for some contrast, you can take a dip in the chilly lake right from the dock. The wooden herbal sauna fills the air with aromas of locally grown heather, rosemary, and birch, awakening your respiratory system. The outdoor hot tub's warm waters and lake views will relax your muscles and allow you to unwind. Lastly, you can retreat to the relaxation room for quiet reflection by the wood-burning fireplace, sipping tea.

116 THE SPA
AT ASHFORD CASTLE

Ashford Castle, F31 CA48 Cong, County Mayo, Ireland

This is the Emerald Isle's best castle spa for utter serenity amid sheer beauty.

The former home of the Guinness family, Ashford Castle in County Mayo is nothing if not grand, and the remarkable spa within is a respite of tranquility. Within the bronze conservatory attached to one side of the castle is a relaxation pool with seated jets and a mesmerizing mural named "The Tree of Life" that showcases Irish Celtic mythology. On the other side of the conservatory, floor-to-ceiling windows offer breathtaking views of Lough Corrib and the gorgeous green castle grounds. Additional facilities include a eucalyptus-infused stone steam room and an authentic hammam, where you can experience an utterly unique treatment that puts an Irish twist on the classic Middle Eastern practice by using locally grown, seaweed-based Voya body-care products to create a soothing wrap and scrub. Or indulge in the Ashford Castle Ritual, performed in one of the five charming treatment rooms overlooking the lough. It begins with a back massage with warmed oil, followed by a nourishing frangipani hair mask and a Nature Bissé facial for radiance, ending with a therapeutic scalp massage, and a pressure-point foot massage.

117 MEZZATORE HOTEL & THERMAL SPA

Via Mezzatorre 23/d, 80075 Forio Naples, Italy

Perched atop a cliff in Ischia, in a 16th-century watchtower overlooking the cerulean Gulf of Naples, Mezzatorre Hotel & Thermal Spa is a peaceful haven designed to restore the senses and re-energize the body, facilitating a journey to your inner self. Ischia is one of the oldest spa destinations in the world, and Mezzatore's Thermal Spa draws inspiration from this rich heritage. The thermal waters, with temperatures reaching 45°C (113°F), flow from the hotel's private spring into two hydrotherapy pools with jets. Additionally, there is a seawater pool, Turkish bath, sauna, sensory showers, and Kneipp pools, featuring a vascular path comprising a hot thermal water pool and a cold seawater pool. Unique facial and body treatments are performed using Ischia's mineral-rich thermal water, including services that utilize mud produced by blending the island's thermal water with volcanic clay. This treatment is believed to be highly effective for ailments such as respiratory pathologies, rheumatism, and dermatitis. Additional beauty and relaxation treatments use products from well-known brands like Biologique Recherche, Augustinus Bader, and Santa Maria Novella.

mezzatorre.com/en/wellness.html   +39 081 986111

118 THE SPA AT FORESTIS

Palmschoß 22, 39042 Brixen, Dolomites, Italy

TO VISIT
BEFORE YOU DIE
BECAUSE

You'll discover the healing powers of alpine trees.

On the wooded slope of Plose Mountain and offering stunning views of Italy's Dolomite Mountains, Forestis takes full advantage of its alpine location to promote health and incorporate high-altitude medicine. At Forestis, all spa treatments are based on a unique concept centered around the region's four trees and their healing properties. These four trees—mountain pine, spruce, larch, and Swiss stone pine—possess various active ingredients, frequencies, and material substances that facilitate effective body regeneration. The Tree Circle Ceremony, a 180-minute experience, allows you to select one of the four tree woods, with the scent of your chosen tree filling the room, while your body is cleansed during a wrapping technique and then massaged with wooden sticks and healing stones corresponding to the chosen tree. Alternatively, you can book the private spa room with views of the Dolomites and indulge in a mountain pine body scrub, a healing wood massage, a steam bath session, and a forest salt bath. Whichever treatment you choose, you can also enjoy a spring-fed, indoor-outdoor stone and wood pool, relax in wooden saunas, practice Wyda (the yoga of the Celts), or unwind in the Silence Rooms overlooking the mountains.

forestis.it/en/luxury-spa-dolomites   +39 0472 521 008

119 LEFAY SPA AT LEFAY RESORT & SPA LAGO DI GARDA

Via Angelo Feltrinelli 136, 25084 Gargnano, Brescia, Italy

TO VISIT
BEFORE YOU DIE
BECAUSE

This resort offers the best of Western and Eastern remedies in a lakeside retreat.

The renowned Lefay Spa Method, used at both Lefay Resort & Spa Lago di Garda and the Dolomites location, combines the principles of traditional Chinese medicine with Western scientific research. This approach employs the five pillars of medical energy diagnosis, treatments, nutrition, phytotherapy, and energy rebalancing to guide targeted wellness programs and its vast array of treatments. With about 100 services on the treatment menu, guests can choose from therapies that span the globe, including non-invasive beauty treatments, energy healing, and medical services. The spa is divided into three areas: the Nature and Fitness area, which consists of a state-of-the-art gym; In Silence and Among the Stars, offering spacious outdoor areas for sporting activities and wellness trails for qi gong and Meridian stretching; and the World of Water and Fire, which consists of swimming pools, four saunas (including one made of olive wood), a hammam, grottos, and small lakes. An adult-only area contains a whirlpool, a Finnish sauna with lake views, experiential showers, and a cool stream and ice pool. The resort is surrounded by 11 hectares of parkland with rolling hills, natural terraces, and olive groves overlooking magnificent Lake Garda.

lagodigarda.lefayresorts.com/
en/lake-garda-spa-and-resort   +39 0365 241 800

120   PALAZZO FIUGGI

Via dei Villini, 34, 03014 Fuiggi Frosinone, Italy

TO VISIT
BEFORE YOU DIE
BECAUSE

Palazzo Fiuggi's legendary healing waters are now complemented by a cutting-edge spa facility.

Situated approximately an hour southeast of Rome, in an area celebrated for its healing mineral waters, Palazzo Fiuggi boasts a world-class spa and medical facility. Blending holistic traditions with advanced Western medicine, the Fiuggi Method retreat provides an integrative approach with a personalized program. You will be assessed before arrival and when you do arrive you'll undergo a reception ritual involving a traditional Turkish hammam bathing session with Fiuggi water and black soap infused with Argan oil, followed by an application of rose water. Throughout your stay, you'll experience tailored health, wellness, fitness, and spa programming, along with nutritious meals and snacks. The extensive Roman Thermae pools, saunas, and Turkish baths are available for lounging. The high-concept spa is at the heart of Palazzo Fiuggi, featuring immaculate marble indoor and outdoor pools and thalassotherapy baths infused with sea minerals. The spa is equipped with advanced facilities, including an MLX i3 Dome for detox treatments that combine far-infrared rays technology with plasma light therapy, as well as a specially designed natural quartz sand bed. Spa treatments include Dead Sea mud wraps, sound healing, and Dr. Barbara Sturm facials.

121 PREIDLHOF LUXURY DOLCE VITA RESORT

Via San Zeno 13 39025, 39025 Naturno, Bolzano, Italy

TO VISIT
BEFORE YOU DIE
BECAUSE

This award-winning, family-owned mountain spa retreat is a holistic wellness getaway.

Since 1966, Preidlhof Luxury Dolce Vita Resort in South Tyrol has tapped into the natural beauty of the surrounding Italian foothills. This award-winning, family-owned mountain spa retreat is renowned for its holistic programs and nine wellness retreats. It offers a wide range of facilities, including a medical spa, a separate nine-room spa center, and its famous Sauna Tower with 16 different saunas, steam rooms, and unique relaxation areas, including the Deep Sea Relaxation Room that replicates the sensation of being underwater through sound and light. With six pools and seven Jacuzzis, including the panoramic Infinity-Solepool providing stunning valley views, the resort provides relaxation at its best. Preidlhof is also connected to the thermal waters in the adjacent town, and underwater massages using thermal water from Kochenmoos are available at the spa. The spa menu encompasses Eastern and Western therapies, such as the Candle Massage, Sound & Quartz, Yaku Shiatsu, Shirodhara, Slow Facial, Kneipp Experience, Shaping Mud, and Dolomitic Sleep Ritual.

122 SPA PACAI AT HOTEL PACAI

Didžioji 7, 01128 Vilnius, Lithuania

TO VISIT
BEFORE YOU DIE
BECAUSE

You'll be enveloped
by Baroque-
style fused with
modernity and
Baltic nature.

Situated in Vilnius's old town, Hotel Pacai is a chic luxury hotel and a member of Design Hotels. The hotel is housed in a beautifully restored Baroque-style building that was once the most magnificent mansion in the Grand Duchy of Lithuania. Downstairs, award-winning Spa Pacai is an intimate urban sanctuary with three treatment rooms, a dry air hammam, sauna, and fitness area. The spa's dark, stylish interior features onyx, Bali wood, marble, granite, and authentic pieces of historic art. The spa's offerings include hammam sessions and various massages and facials that use Biologique Recherche products. You can also indulge in spa rituals like the Spa Pacai Signature Ritual for Body and Soul, which begins in the sauna to relax the muscles and is followed by a four-hand full-body massage using birch rod leaves in the candlelit VIP treatment room.

123 BRITANNIA SPA AT BRITANNIA HOTEL

Dronningensgate 5, 7011 Trondheim, Norway

You can bask in luxury near the Arctic Circle.

Britannia Hotel is known for being the world's most northerly grand dame hotel. This member of the Leading Hotels of the World originally opened in 1870, and underwent a a $160 million refurbishment before reopening in 2019 with the addition of a brand new spa. The well-appointed space has six treatment rooms, a heated indoor lap pool, a sauna, steam room, an ice bath, a Jacuzzi, a gym, an infrared cabin, and a tranquil relaxation room. The extensive treatment menu offers a range of Eastern and Western therapies, including Thai massage, tui na, physiotherapy, Elemis facials, and the signature Stress Busting Back Massage, which features targeted techniques to release knots and soothe tight muscles. There's also a full line of kids and teen treatments, ensuring that everyone in the family can enjoy the experience.

britannia.no/en/spa   +47 738 00 800

124 THE SPA AT SOLSTRAND HOTEL & SPA

Solstrandveien 200, 5200 Os, Norway

TO VISIT
BEFORE YOU DIE
BECAUSE

You'll revel in the stunning beauty of the fjord at this Norwegian retreat.

With its magnificent view of the fjord and the mountains just 18 miles from Bergen, Solstrand Hotel & Spa has attracted guests from around the world since 1896, when it originally opened as a seawater pool. Today, in addition to the hotel, it is home to a modern spa complex with an indoor pool, a heated outdoor pool, a therapy pool with massage jets and loungers, a Finnish sauna, a steam room, a sanarium, and a cold plunge. For an authentic Nordic experience, take a dip in the pristine fjord after enjoying a sauna session. The spa treatments are Nordic inspired, including the 80-minute Nordic Zen, involving a body scrub, facial cleansing and facial massage, hot juniper oil application, and hot stone massage. Swedish spa guru Kerstin Florian supplies the products for the facials, mud wraps, and algae treatments.

125 THE SPA AT THE WELL

Kongeveien 65, 1412 Sofiemyr, Norway

A mere 15 minutes from Oslo, The Well is a massive wellness paradise with the largest spa in Scandinavia, covering more than 113,000 square feet. The spa combines Nordic and Japanese bathing traditions, featuring four separate steam rooms, ten different pools, hot tubs, and showers, including a hidden hot spring bath, a waterfall cave, and a Japanese-style onsen. The Well's highlight is the nine diverse saunas of varying degrees, humidities, and styles, such as a laconium with lights mimicking the aurora borealis, a Finnish sauna, and Japanese and meditation saunas with windows facing onto a Japanese-style zen garden. The spa master enhances your experience with *aufguss*, a fragrant infusion made of ice balls and essential oils that he places atop the sauna heater. He then waves a towel to distribute the fragrant hot air around the sauna, to the accompaniment of music. The spa has a robust menu of massages, Babor and Elemis facials, and body scrubs and wraps, ensuring a diverse range of pampering options.

thewell.no/en/spa   +47 480 44 888

126 LAUREA SPA AT SAVOY PALACE

Avenida do Infante Nº 25, 9004-542 Funchal, Madeira, Portugal

Portugal's Pearl of the Atlantic inspires the treatments at this verdant spa.

Drawing inspiration from Madeira's mystical Laurissilva Forest bursting with vivid colors, the Laurea Spa uses local ingredients and techniques. Tucked within the grand Savoy Palace, a member of the Leading Hotels of the World, the spa features treatments like the signature Laurea Massage, which utilizes Madeira's hot and cold volcanic stones to increase and stimulate circulation, relieve muscle tension, and reduce stress and fatigue. The Power Ritual by Sodashi is another exquisite treatment, beginning with a deep facial cleansing with mineral-rich Argillite clay and hot compresses. This is followed by a facial massage combined with either a décolleté/neck and shoulder massage, a head massage, or a foot massage, all while a customized gel face mask is applied. Post-treatment, you can lounge in the spa's sauna, hot tub, steam room, sensory showers, halotherapy room, Kneipp walk, heated indoor pool, and nature-inspired relaxation room. A Champagne nail bar by renowned podiatrist Margaret Dabbs, a beauty salon, and a gym complete the spa's offerings.

savoysignature.com/
savoypalacehotel/en/spa/laurea-spa   +351 291 213 000

127 THE SPA AT OCTANT FURNAS

Avenida Dr. Manuel de Arriaga, Furnas,
9675-022 São Miguel, Portugal

TO VISIT
BEFORE YOU DIE
BECAUSE

Volcanic hot springs and other local delicacies are utilized to their full healing effect.

Octant Furnas is arguably the best spa hotel in the Azores archipelago, located in São Miguel's hot spring town of Furnas. This hotel is built around naturally occurring thermal waters, which have been a source of healing for Azoreans and visitors for centuries. The spa offers a series of 24-hour-accessible indoor-outdoor thermal pools and a hydrotherapy circuit that draws from the natural springs, as well as a sauna, laconium, Turkish bath, and aromatic showers. The spa also features ten treatment rooms with a menu of scrubs, massages, and facials that incorporate ingredients such as olive oil, rosemary, salt, locally grown green tea, seaweed, cacao, and coffee. The mouth-watering Pineapple Breeze, a scrub of brown sugar and locally grown pineapple, will leave you smelling like a piña colada, while the Furnas Power consists of a massage with volcanic stones, precious stones, and a clay wrap. The spa also offers Ayurvedic therapies, shiatsu, reflexology, and flotation beds, if you're after the lulling motion of ocean waves without getting wet.

furnas.octanthotels.com/
en/spa-and-thermae   +351 296 249 200

128 ESTORIL WELLNESS CENTRE AT PALÁCIO ESTORIL HOTEL

Rua Particular 2769, 504 Estoril, Cascais, Portugal

TO VISIT
BEFORE YOU DIE
BECAUSE

It's a comprehensive medically based wellness center combined with an established Asian spa brand, all in one place.

Located just 20 minutes from Lisbon, the Palácio Estoril is home to the illustrious Estoril Wellness Centre. The Centre, which offers comprehensive health and wellbeing therapies, has a staff comprised of physiotherapists, masseurs, osteopaths, nutritionists, and integrative/preventative medical practitioners. Services include advanced aesthetic and clinical treatments, such as radiofrequency, anti-cellulite/slimming treatments, and unique steam treatments such as Bertholaix, which targets water vapor to relieve tension and aches in the shoulders, hips, and spine. The Vichy shower massage involves lying under high pressure jets while a therapist massages you with essential oils. The spa's vast facilities include a dynamic heated pool, a therapeutic swimming pool, a Jacuzzi, saunas, steam rooms, and a Turkish bath. A fitness center with four movement studios for activities such as Pilates, yoga, tae bo, and dance is also available. Additionally, Palácio Estoril hosts the award-winning Banyan Tree Spa, which features luxurious treatments based on holistic Asian healing philosophies overlooking manicured gardens with sea views. Full programs from three to seven days are available, offering comprehensive medical, physical, and wellness treatments.

129   SIX SENSES SPA AT SIX SENSES DOURO VALLEY

Quinta de Vale Abraão, 5100-758 Samodães Lamego, Portugal

You'll be healed and pampered amid rolling, vineyard-covered hills.

Portuguese tradition meets the elements of water, stone, and wood in a supreme setting at Six Senses Spa at Six Senses Douro Valley. Your wellness journey begins with a non-invasive wellness screening that measures your key biomarkers to help tailor a wellness program just for you. The spa uses the latest technology, from skin analysis to biohacking, to create a personalized wellness experience. In addition to a range of massages and facials, the spa offers state-of-the-art treatments like Cell Gym Oxygen Therapy, Movement Restoration, a full line of Ayurvedic therapies, and the signature Dream Catcher, featuring a full body massage with vanilla and oud CBD oil, a body wrap, and a facial with CBD products, all aimed at promoting a peaceful slumber. The spa has an indoor pool with floor-to-ceiling garden views, underwater sound therapy, and massage jets. The Vitality Suite offers a classic sauna, an infrared sauna, a steam room, a laconium, an herbal sauna, and a vitality pool.

sixsenses.com/en/resorts/
douro-valley/wellness-spa   +351 254 660 600

130 SHA WELLNESS CLINIC

Carrer del Verderol 5, 03581 L'Albir, Alicante, Spain

TO VISIT
BEFORE YOU DIE
BECAUSE

It's a pioneering
wellness retreat
perched on the
Mediterranean
coast.

A pioneering clinical luxury wellness resort, the SHA Wellness Clinic takes an integrated approach to health, guided by a mission of helping people live longer and better lives. The clinic's location in the middle of the stunning Sierra Helada Natural Park on the sparkling Mediterranean will make your stay even more enjoyable. The SHA Method, developed and overseen by eminent experts, integrates eight holistic disciplines and offers programs ranging from four to 21 days that focus on healthy aging, detox, and rebalancing. Highlights at SHA include sleep medicine consultation and solutions, biologic age evaluation, and transformative breathing treatments. This unique approach integrates inventive, scientific treatments with the best of Eastern medicine to promote wellbeing.

131 SIX SENSES SPA AT SIX SENSES IBIZA

Camí de Sa Torre, 71, 07810 Sant Joan de Labritja, Balearic Islands, Ibiza, Spain

TO VISIT
BEFORE YOU DIE
BECAUSE

Advanced scientific research and ancient philosophies merge to enhance wellness and longevity.

Ibiza, known for its vibrant nightlife, is also home to one of the world's best spas. The Six Senses Spa at Six Senses Ibiza takes a high-tech approach to wellness and crafts tailored program for its guests. The spa offers personalized treatments provided by global practitioners and expert yogic masters, along with functional fitness and anti-aging remedies. Covering nearly 130,000 square feet, the expansive spa includes a steam room, a hammam, a caldarium hot bath, and a tropical rain shower. Outdoors, there are massage catacombs with direct access to organic gardens that grow ingredients for the spa and Alchemy Bar. Signature treatments include the 90-minute After Party Detox, which consists of a tangy citrus body scrub, a stimulating, full body massage, and a calming facial massage using gua sha tools. The 528 Hz Face Massage uses a tuning fork at the 528 Hz frequency, believed to assist with DNA repair, lymphatic flow, circulation, and muscle tension relief. The RoseBar offers customized longevity treatments and personal guidance combining cutting-edge science with spirituality to combat ageing.

sixsenses.com/en/resorts/ibiza/wellness-spa   +34 871 00 88 75

132 THE SPA AT KOSTA BODA ART HOTEL

Stora vägen 75, 365 43 Kosta, Sweden

Where else can you be massaged with glass from the Kingdom of Crystal?

Kosta Boda Art Hotel combines the beauty of Sweden's Kingdom of Crystal with a design hotel concept and a showroom for the brand's art crystal. The hotel is a showcase for the famous designers of Orrefors and Kosta Boda—including a display at the bottom of the indoor pool. The hotel's spa stands out by incorporating the stunning crystal into some of its treatments. The Art Glass Feeling ritual is an exclusive body treatment in which warm Swedish glass is used for a massage. This treatment also includes a full body peel, softening, and a revitalizing body mask, all followed by a face and scalp massage. The treatment culminates in a warm shower, after which guests get to choose a glass gift from Åsa Jungnelius's "Make Up" series to take home.

133 LOKA BRUNN

712 94 Grythyttan, Sweden

You'll experience the Swedish healing tradition of gyttja mud beds and pine needle baths.

Welcome to Loka Brunn, where the air is clear and you're surrounded by the wooded Lokadalen Valley in Northern Sweden. For hundreds of years, Swedes (including Swedish royalty) have ventured to Loka Brunn to avail themselves of the healing atmosphere, and there are more than 50 structures at the charming site, many dating back to the 1700s. Today, there are 11 indoor and outdoor pools with grand chandeliers overhead, three saunas and steam rooms, and an array of unique therapies. The signature gyttja treatments, rooted in Swedish healing traditions that go back to the 18th century, are a must-try. Gyttja, a mud formed from peat decay, is collected from behind Loka church and mixed with water to create a kind of mud used in the therapies. The Lokas Brunnskur treatment involves a warm gyttja bed, a back massage, and a hot bath with local pine needle oil made onsite. Other treatments include massages, facials, and body scrubs, using Swedish organic brand Kerstin Florian products. Leave time to snuggle up by the fireplace in the Gläntan relaxation room and take in the spectacular views of Norra Loken.

134 BÜRGENSTOCK ALPINE SPA AT BÜRGENSTOCK RESORT LAKE LUCERNE

Bürgenstock 17, 6363 Obbürgen, Switzerland

The Swiss mountain and lake views are unmatched at this luxurious spa.

Stretching across more than 60 hectares, the Bürgenstock Resort Lake Lucerne is a luxury resort destination with jaw-dropping scenery of Lake Lucerne and the Alps. The resort's Bürgenstock Alpine Spa covers more than 100,000 square feet with five pools, including an outdoor infinity pool with panoramic views of the Swiss landscape. It also offers four saunas with lake views, an Alpine steambath, relaxation lounges, and 13 treatment rooms. You can indulge in facial and body treatments by high-end European skincare brands that include Dr. Burgener, 111 Skin, Amra, KOS Paris, and Dr. Barbara Sturm. The Amra Golden Opulence is a standout treatment that involves a full body cleansing and exfoliation, followed by a massage with 24-karat gold body oil, and then a final infusion of Amra's Precious Drops of Gold.

burgenstockresort.com/
en/spa/buergenstock-alpine-spa   +41 41 612 60 00

135 THE SPA AND TAMINA THERMAE AT GRAND RESORT BAD RAGAZ

Bernhard-Simonstrasse 20, 7310 Bad Ragaz, Switzerland

TO VISIT
BEFORE YOU DIE
BECAUSE

An 800-year-old thermal spring is the source of wellness here.

The Grand Resort Bad Ragaz, located in the foothills of the Swiss Alps, is home to the Tamina Therme and a vast wellness zone. The resort's history dates back to 1242 when the healing waters of the Tamina Gorge were first discovered. Today, these warm mineral waters remain highly regarded, and the entire spa is centered around their healing powers. The resort's wellness zone has eight indoor and outdoor thermal pools, including hydromassage pools, a counter-current pool, and the grand Helena Bath, which dates back to the 19th century. The gorgeous public baths, Tamina Thermae, include access to Sauna World, which has Finnish saunas, a Latvian pirts sauna, and Switzerland's largest infusion sauna, a Kelo pine sauna. A highlight is witnessing the impressive performances by the Ragaz *aufguss* sauna masters. A specialty of the spa is the four rituals inspired by the haki—The Art of Touch philosophy, which includes one performed amid the thermal waters. The spa also offers Babor facials, a variety of massages, and numerous body treatments.

resortragaz.ch/en/health-and-wellness/
wellness-area/tamina-therme   +41 81 303 30 30

136 THE DOLDER SPA AT THE DOLDER GRAND

Kurhausstrasse 65, 8032 Zurich, Switzerland

This spa represents the finest in Japanese and Swiss wellness traditions.

The Dolder Grand, often referred to as Zurich's "Castle on the Hill", is an opulent and art-filled hotel. Its 43,000-square-foot Dolder Spa, designed by renowned spa master Sylvia Sepielli, showcases a unique blend of Japanese and Swiss elements in its design. The state-of-the-art facility boasts an 82-foot indoor swimming pool made of Italian Bisazza mosaic, cold-water plunge pools, a sanarium, a snow zone, Japanese-inspired Sunaboros filled with warm pebbles, and an outdoor pool and terrace with views of the Swiss Alps. Saunas, steam baths, kotasu foot baths, aroma pools, and a meditation area crowned with a gorgeous mirror mosaic cupola complete the spa's offerings. Eighteen treatment rooms and two private spa suites overlooking Lake Zurich host massages, facials, and holistic rituals that promote relaxation and rejuvenation.

thedoldergrand.com/en/spa   +41 44 456 60 00

137 TSCHUGGEN BERGOASE SPA AT TSCHUGGEN GRAND HOTEL

Tschuggentorweg 1, 7050 Arosa, Switzerland

Switzerland's dramatic mountain peaks provide the perfect backdrop for the ultra-modern Tschuggen Bergoase Spa at the Tschuggen Grand Hotel, a member of the Leading Hotels of the World. Situated in the Alpine region of Arosa, the 54,000-square-foot wellness center is built directly into the surrounding mountain, where a four-story retreat awaits. Designed by Swiss architect Mario Botta, the spa features one-of-a-kind sail-shaped windows made from steel and glass, allowing the sky and mountains to reach the furthest corners of the spa and flood the four levels with light.

The spa consists of an indoor-outdoor pool with undulating granite walls and water falls, plunge pools, saunas, and steam rooms that are the perfect antidote to a day spent on the slopes. The impressive treatment menu includes locally influenced therapies, such as the Swiss Stone Mountain Pine Massage, which incorporates wooden pine rollers, as well as cutting-edge technologies and scientific approaches to wellness.

tschuggencollection.ch/en/hotel/
tschuggen-grand-hotel/spa   +41 81 378 95 95

138 THE BOTHY BY WILDSMITH AT HECKFIELD PLACE

Heckfield Place, RG27 0LD Heckfield, Hook, United Kingdom

TO VISIT
BEFORE YOU DIE
BECAUSE

You'll feel connected to nature amid striking architecture that fosters a genuinely peaceful atmosphere.

Heckfield Place, a delightful 250-year-old Georgian family home transformed into a boutique hotel in Hampshire, revealed a brand-new wellness space in partnership with British skincare brand Wildsmith Skin in 2023. The Bothy by Wildsmith is discreetly hidden beyond a secret door within the original walled garden of the house. Inside is a 17,000-square-foot space seamlessly connected to its natural surroundings. It features fossilized limestone floors and sinks, antique Hampshire bricks that are part of the original Bothy's restoration, and 29,434 hand-laid tiles in the Waters, a chlorine-free pool infused with natural mineral ions of copper, silver, zinc, aluminum, and gold. You can explore the Oak Terrace, home to outdoor hydrotherapy and thermal experiences, including a sauna, steam room, experiential shower, and a cold water bucket shower. The six treatment rooms are where you'll enjoy massages, facials, reiki, bodywork, and more, including the signature Wildsmith Time treatment, which incorporates kinesiology principles and a therapeutic massage using essential oil blends specifically formulated to match circadian rhythms and the time of day. Each treatment includes craniosacral holds, an abdominal massage, and foot zone reflex therapy.

139 ESPA LIFE AT CORINTHIA LONDON

Whitehall Place, SW1A 2BD London, United Kingdom

TO VISIT
BEFORE YOU DIE
BECAUSE

This is one of the largest, most opulent spas in London.

Espa Life at Corinthia London is one of London's most opulent spas and provides an immediate escape from the hubbub of the city. Spanning four floors, the spa encompasses 17 treatment rooms, including a private spa suite, and a calming Thermal Floor that houses an elegant indoor swimming pool, a vitality pool, an amphitheater sauna, an ice fountain, marble heated loungers, and private sleep pods for a true retreat. The extensive treatment menu is categorized into themes such as Nurture, Purify, Vitality, Reflection, Resilience, and Wellness Therapies, offering services ranging from body wraps and Theragun massages to cryotherapy facials and HydraFacials, employing cutting-edge technology.

     espalifeatcorinthia.com   +44 20 7321 3050

140   THE SPA
AT COWORTH PARK

Coworth Park, Blacknest Road,
SL5 7SE Ascot Berkshire, United Kingdom

TO VISIT
BEFORE YOU DIE
BECAUSE

**The British
countryside offers a
picturesque setting
for an award-
winning spa.**

Set in the serene Berkshire countryside, the posh Coworth Park is an idyl-lic hideaway with an award-winning destination spa. The Spa at Coworth Park, situated in a standalone building within well-manicured grounds, is designed with natural and organic materials, ample natural daylight, and vast parkland views. The facilities include eight treatment rooms, a relaxa-tion room, the Spatisserie café, and an indoor pool adorned with amethyst sculptures. The spa offers a wide range of services utilizing three premi-um skincare product lines: Germaine de Capuccini from Spain, Valmont from Sweden, and Ishga Organic from Scotland. A standout treatment is the Hebridean Sound treatment by Ishga Organic, inspired by the sounds of water and the musical traditions of the Scottish archipelago. This unique treatment begins with a seaweed foot ritual, followed by a meditation se-quence using singing bowls, a full body Balinese-inspired massage, and warmed ishga oil poured gently over the forehead and scalp, followed by a face massage that stimulates your pressure points. The treatment culmi-nates with a singing bowl awakening.

dorchestercollection.com/
ascot/coworth-park/wellness   +44 1344 876 600

141 SPA VILLAGE BATH AT THE GAINSBOROUGH BATH SPA

Beau Street, 1QY Bath BA1, England, United Kingdom

TO VISIT
BEFORE YOU DIE
BECAUSE

Indulging in the thermal waters of Bath is an unforgettable bucket-list experience.

Bath's mineral springs have been revered for centuries, and in 43 AD the Romans constructed a complex surrounding the springs. The mineral-rich thermal waters were already cherished by the residing Celts, making the city a magnet for those seeking healing and calming properties. The Gainsborough Bath Spa is the only hotel with direct access to these natural thermal waters. The spa revives the ancient practice of social bathing, offering guests a one-hour Bath Circuit, featuring time in three different pools that are reminiscent of a Roman bathhouse. You can also access traditional and infrared saunas, a steam room, an ice alcove, and elegant relaxation areas. Massages, body treatments, and facials take place in the 11 treatment rooms, including a private suite with its own thermal bathing area.

thegainsboroughbathspa.co.uk/
pages/spa-village-bath.html

+44 1225 358 888

142 THE LANESBOROUGH CLUB & SPA

Lanesborough Place 2, SW1X 7TA London,
England, United Kingdom

You'll join London's elite at the city's most exclusive health and wellness club.

The award-winning Lanesborough Club & Spa, an upscale private members' fitness and health club in London's Belgravia, is one of the city's most exclusive venues. The club combines luxury club and lounge elements with top-tier fitness, wellness, and spa facilities. The grand reception areas lead to quieter central spa spaces with a design inspired by the ceremonial spaces of the Roman Bath Spa. Silk wallpapers, leather upholstery, marble and oak furnishings, and bronze accents create a truly lavish ambiance. Spa facilities include spacious thermal suites with hot tubs, steam baths, and showers surrounding the elegant spa lounge and treatment rooms. The peaceful indoor hydro-pool is lined with comfortable loungers and provides an idyllic escape from the city. A variety of treatments are available, featuring products like Tata Harper, ila, and Royal Fern. These services range from the ila CBD Immersion to the Tata Harper Grounding Yogic Facial, along with an extensive Advanced Aesthetics Menu offering treatments such as HydraFacial, Microneedling with Dermapen, and Fat Dissolving Treatment with Lipo Lab PPC. For a truly regal experience, try treatments using precious gems, such as the pearl and jasmine salt body scrub or an amethyst gel body wrap.

lanesboroughclubandspa.com/the-club-spa   +44 20 7333 7064

143   THE FLOATING SPA AT MONKEY ISLAND ESTATE

Bray-On-Thames, SL6 2EE Bray,
Maidenhead, England, United Kingdom

TO VISIT
BEFORE YOU DIE
BECAUSE

This spa will rock
you into a state of
total tranquility.

Inspired by the 17th-century Apothecaries' Barge that was moored off the River Thames at Chelsea Physic Garden, where people sought cures and marveled at herbal remedies, the Floating Spa at Monkey Island Estate offers an utterly distinctive spa experience. The custom-crafted barge is anchored on the banks of Monkey Island Estate, located on a secluded forested island in the River Thames, near the historic village of Bray. The bright blue boat features three treatment rooms, a cozy wheelhouse reception area, and the Elixir Bar. The treatment menu may be concise but is thoughtfully designed, with the signature Monks Elixir treatment paying homage to the 12th-century Augustinian monks who settled along the river and established fishing ponds at the north end of Monkey Island. The treatment begins with an elixir tasting of a monk-brewed tonic (Chartreuse, D.O.M Benedictine, or Frangelico), followed by a full body massage using a house-cured herbal oil infused with arnica, angelica, melisse, and frankincense. Warm herbal pouches are placed on your joints to relieve stiffness as the gentle rocking of the boat lulls you to total relaxation.

monkeyislandestate.co.uk/pages/spa.html   +44 1628 623 400

144 THE SPA SANCTUARY AT GWINGANNA

Syndicate Road 192, 4228 Tallebudgera Valley,
Queensland, Australia

TO VISIT
BEFORE YOU DIE
BECAUSE

The largest spa in the Southern Hemisphere will simultaneously awe and rejuvenate you.

Nestled within the forest of Queensland's Gold Coast, the award-winning eco-retreat of Gwinganna is a renowned wellness destination frequented by celebrities. The tree-encircled Spa Sanctuary, the largest in the Southern Hemisphere, offers three wings, 33 treatment rooms, the upper-level Whisper Lounge, an amethyst crystal steam room, and an outdoor monsoon shower. The exquisite indoor-outdoor design centers around three ancient eucalyptus trees and circular structures radiating from them. The spa, constructed with salvaged timber, is entirely self-sufficient in water consumption, relying solely on collected runoff water. The spa's treatments range from organic facials to Ayurvedic body wraps, Lomi Lomi and lymphatic drainage massages, as well as astrology, reiki, acupuncture, naturopath consultations, and equine therapy.

145   SPA KINARA AT LONGITUDE 131

Yulara Drive, 0872 Yulara, Northern Territory, Australia

TO VISIT
BEFORE YOU DIE
BECAUSE

You'll be immersed in healing energies in one of the world's most sacred places.

Longitude 131, situated in the heart of the Australian outback near Uluru, offers a luxurious lodge experience. The property's Spa Kinara is designed in the style of an indigenous *wiltja* (shelter), and is deeply connected to Aboriginal customs and healing traditions. Working closely with the local Ngaanyatjarra Pitjantjatjara Yankunytjatjara (NPY) Lands Women's Council, the spa incorporates traditional healing practices into its therapies. Each treatment begins with a healing smoking ceremony using bush botanicals and culminates with an outdoor rain shower. The spa uses native ingredients such as Kakadu plum, quandongs, desert lime, Australian yellow clay, nutrient-rich desert salts, and *irmangka-irmangka* (scented emu bush). In the Ngangkari Program run by the NPY, women make a balm using irmangka-irmangka, which is also featured in the spa's offerings.

146   SPA QUALIA

Whitsunday Boulevard 20, 4802 Hamilton Island,
Queensland, Australia

**TO VISIT
BEFORE YOU DIE
BECAUSE**

**Spa Qualia offers
ultimate serenity in
the midst of one
of the world's
natural wonders.**

Located at the northernmost tip of Hamilton Island, surrounded by the Great Barrier Reef, Spa Qualia is already a sanctuary. At the heart of the resort is Spa Qualia, offering even more bliss. The spa uses all-natural, Australian-made products, including brands such as Sodashi, LaGaia Unedited, People4Ocean, and Hunter Lab. The treatments draw inspiration from indigenous traditions. Signature Spa Qualia experiences include the Driftaway Sensory Journey, the Qualia Essence, and the three-hour Whitsunday Escape, which entails a full body exfoliation and mud wrap, a private rain shower, an aromatic full body massage, heat therapy, a hair and scalp treatment, and a marine mineral facial. The spa also offers Roman-style mineral baths, reflexology, and an abdominal massage aimed at re-energizing digestive organs.

147   FIJI BEACH SPA AT THE JEAN-MICHEL COUSTEAU RESORT

Lesiaceva Point Road, Savusavu, Fiji

TO VISIT BEFORE YOU DIE BECAUSE

This destination offers a chance to experience the natural bliss and traditional healing practices of Fiji.

A stay at the Jean-Michel Cousteau Resort promises a beautiful natural setting and eco-luxury accommodation. In addition to various underwater and land adventures, the resort offers wellness-focused activities. These include internet-free periods, restorative yoga sessions, meditation, a Fijian medicine walk, wellness juice shots at breakfast based on ancient Fijian recipes, and traditional Fijian spa treatments at the Fiji Beach Spa. The open-air treatment *bures* are beachfront, allowing guests to immerse themselves in the soothing sounds of ocean waves. For a unique experience, request a treatment with Viri Marivale, the head spa therapist, who hails from a long line of Fijian healers. She incorporates Fijian Reiki and local botanicals into her treatments, utilizing pure local Fijian ingredients including cold-pressed coconut oil, raw sugar, ylang-ylang, cacao, honey, nuts, and spices.

148 DEEP OCEAN SPA AT INTERCONTINENTAL BORA BORA RESORT & THALASSO SPA

Motu Piti Aau, 98730 Bora Bora, French Polynesia

TO VISIT
BEFORE YOU DIE
BECAUSE

The therapeutic benefits of the Pacific Ocean envelop you from all sides at this extraordinary spa.

The Deep Ocean Spa at InterContinental Bora Bora Resort & Thalasso Spa offers a unique blend of therapeutic treatments and stunning surroundings. The spa features glass-bottomed, over-water treatment rooms boasting immersive water views of the surrounding ocean. It is the South Pacific's first thalassotherapy center to use seawater drawn from the Pacific Ocean.
The spa's facilities include multisensory outdoor whirlpools, various steam baths and showers, and the opportunity to gaze into the colorful ocean beneath. Choose from a range of treatments, including a deep-sea hydro-massage bath with chromatherapy, a traditional Polynesian Taurumi massage, or a pearl rain massage that involves a massage with oils under a deep-sea water shower.

thalasso.intercontinental.com/
spa-and-wellness/deep-ocean-spa +68 9 4060 7700

149   VARUA TE ORA POLYNESIAN SPA AT THE BRANDO

Arue, 98702 Tetiaroa, French Polynesia

TO VISIT
BEFORE YOU DIE
BECAUSE

You can immerse yourself in Polynesian wellness culture amidst breathtaking natural beauty.

The Brando is an exquisite luxury resort surrounded by pristine beauty on the private atoll of Tetiaroa in French Polynesia. Varua Te Ora Polynesian Spa is a haven of calm and natural splendor. The spa features elevated pathways through tropical foliage, leading to secluded spaces for relaxation, meditation, contemplation, and treatment. Over-pond pavilion suites and Fare Manu, a canopy suite perched 20 feet high above the trees, offer unique settings for massages and therapies. The spa even provides an Ice-Cold Deep-Sea Water Bath, allowing guests to immerse themselves in seawater drawn from the depths of 3,018 feet in the Pacific Ocean.

thebrando.com/spa-wellness   +68 9 4086 6360

150 ARO-HĀ WELLNESS RETREAT

Station Valley Road 33, 9372 Glenorchy, New Zealand

Here you can experience *kia ora* (have life) in a mindful way.

Set against the stunning backdrop of New Zealand's Lake Wakatipu and the snow-capped alps, Aro-Hā Wellness Resort offers a mindful and holistic approach to wellness. With only 20 minimalist rooms, the retreat provides guests with activities like yoga, strength classes, meditation, sub-alpine hiking, nutritious dining, cold/hot therapy, daily massages, and meaningful rest over six or eight days. The Obsidian Spa is the onsite facility offering traditional and infrared saunas, hot and cold plunges for contrast therapy, and massage treatment rooms for deep tissue massages. The combination of contrast therapy and therapeutic massages aims to repair muscles and induce a state of deep calm and tranquility.

© Photos

p.10-11 Mark Williams – Sanctuary Retreats / p.12 Courtesy of La Mamounia / p.13 Courtesy of Royal Mansour / p.14 Courtesy of Babylonstoren / p.15-17 Courtesy of Royal Malewane / p.18 Courtesy of The Twelve Apostles Hotel & Spa / p.19 Courtesy of The Ocean Spa BVI / p.20 Courtesy of Fairmont Banff Springs / p.21 Courtesy of Mountain Trek / p.22-23 CCO Productions – Photographer Chris Oliver / p.24-25 Courtesy of Bota Bota / p.26-27 Courtesy of Tierra Chiloé Hotel & Spa / p.28 Courtesy of Four Seasons Peninsula Papagayo / p.29 Courtesy of The Retreat / p.30-33 Courtesy of Nayara Springs / p.34 Courtesy of Auberge Resorts Collection / p.35 Courtesy of Casa de Campo / p.36 Courtesy of Pikaia Lodge / p.37 Courtesy of Half Moon / p.38-39 Courtesy of One&Only Resorts / p.40-43 Courtesy of Chablé Yucatan / p.44-47 Courtesy of Rosewood Mayakoba / p.48 Courtesy of Rancho La Puerta / p.49-50 Courtesy of Montage Los Cabos / p.51 Courtesy of Tambo del Inka, A Luxury Collection Resort, Valle Sagrada / p.52-55 Jose Ruiz Photography / p.56-57 Courtesy of QC Terme NY / p.58 Courtesy of The Greenwich Hotel / p.59-61 Michael Kleinberg / p.62-63 Courtesy of Fredrika Stjarne for Shou Sugi Ban House / p.64-65 Courtesy of Equinox Hotels / p.66-67 Stuart Thurkill / p.68 Courtesy of Miraval Arizona / p.69-71 Courtesy of Mohonk Mountain House / p.72-73 Courtesy of Four Seasons Philadelphia / p.74 Courtesy of Faena Hotel Miami Beach / p.75-77 Courtesy of Mii Amo / p.78 Courtesy of Four Seasons Resort Maui at Wailea / p.79 Courtesy of 1 Hotel Hanalei Bay / p.80-82 Courtesy of Sensei Lanai, A Four Seasons Resort / p.83 Courtesy of Castle Hot Springs / p.84 Courtesy of Fairmont Century Plaza / p.84 Courtesy of The Ranch Malibu / p.85 Courtesy of Auberge Resorts Collection / p.86 Courtesy of The Boca Raton / p.87-89 Courtesy of Omni Grove Park Inn / p.90-91 Courtesy of Cal-a-Vie / p.92-93 Courtesy of Dunton Destinations / p.94-95 Gordon Gregory / p.96 Bryan Peck, courtesy of Inns of Aurora Resort & Spa p.97-99 Courtesy of Inn of the Five Graces / p.100 Courtesy of Ten Thousand Waves / p.101 Courtesy of Ojo Caliente / p.102-103 Courtesy of Lake Austin Spa Resort / p.104 Courtesy of Amangiri / p.105 Courtesy of Banyan Tree Ringha / p.106 Courtesy of PuXuan Hotel and Spa / p.107 Courtesy of Capella Tufu Bay / p.108-109 Courtesy of Amandayan / p.110 Courtesy of Rosewood Hong Kong / p.111 Courtesy of The Peninsula Hong Kong / p.112 Courtesy of Ananda in the Himalayas / p.113 Courtesy of The Leela Palace Udaipur / p.114 Courtesy of Six Senses Vana / p.115 Courtesy of COMO Shambhala Estate / p.116-117 Courtesy of NIHI Sumba Island / p.118 Courtesy of Capella Ubud / p.119 Courtesy of Aman Kyoto / p.120 Courtesy of Hotel The Mitsui Kyoto / p. 121 Courtesy of Hoshino Resorts / p.122 Courtesy of Rosewood Luang Prabang / p.123 Courtesy of Sunway Hotels / p.124-125 Courtesy of Ritz-Carlton Langkawi / p.126-129 Courtesy of Anantara Kihavah Maldives Villas / p.130-131 Courtesy of Joali Being / p.132 Courtesy of The Chedi Muscat / p.133-135 Courtesy of Zulal Wellness Resort by Chiva-Som / p.136 Courtesy of Spa 1899 Donginbi / p.137 Courtesy of WE Hotel / p.138 Courtesy of Anantara Chiang Mai / p.139 Courtesy of Chiva-Som / p.140 Courtesy of Rakxa / p.141 Courtesy of Cagaloglu Hammam / p.142 Courtesy of Hurrem Sultan Hammam / p. 143 Courtesy of Six Senses Kaplankaya / p.144-145 Courtesy of Qasr Al Sarab by Anantara / p.146 Courtesy of Atlantis the Royal / p.147 Courtesy of Mandarin Oriental / p.148 Michael Huber, courtesy of SPA-Hotel Jagdhof / p.149-151 Courtesy of Rogner Bad Blumau © Hundertwasser Architekturprojekt / p.152-155 Courtesy of Stanglwirt / p.156-157 Courtesy of Energia Eco-Spa and Enterprise Estonia / p.158-159 Courtesy of Les Sources de Caudalie / p.160 Franck Juery, courtesy of Le Relais Bernard Loiseau / p.161-163 George Apostolidis / p.164 David Oliver / p.165 Courtesy of Le Bristol / p.166-167 Mr. Tripper / p.169-169 CARASANA Bäderbetriebe GmbH / p.170-173 Courtesy of Lanserhof Sylt / p.174-175 Courtesy of Schloss Elmau / p.176 Courtesy of Euphoria Retreat / p.177-179 Yiorgos Kordakis / p.180 Courtesy of Andronis Arcadia / p.181 Courtesy of Andronis Concept Wellness Resort / p.182 Courtesy of Magma Resort Santorini, The Unbound Collection by Hyatt / p.183 Courtesy of Vedema, A Luxury Collection Resort / p.185-185 Courtesy of Calilo / p.186-187 Courtesy of Four Seasons Astir Palace Hotel Athens / p.188 Jack Hardy, courtesy of Corinthia Budapest / p.189-191 Courtesy of Széchenyi Baths / p.192 Courtesy of Krauma Geothermal Baths / p.193 Courtesy of Bjorbodin / p.194-197 Courtesy of Sky Lagoon by Pursuit / p.198 Courtesy of Finn Lough / p.199 Courtesy of Ashford Castle / p.200 Courtesy of Pellicano Hotels / p.201 Courtesy of FORESTIS / p.202-203 Courtesy of Lefay Resort & Spa, Lago di Garda / p.204 Courtesy of Palazzo Fiuggi / p.205 Tyson Sadlo – Herd Represented, courtesy of Palazzo Fiuggi / p.206 Courtesy of Preidlhof Luxury Dolce Vita Resort / p.207 Courtesy of Hotel Pacai / p. 208 Dreyer + Hensley / p.209-211 Courtesy of Solstrand Hotel & Spa / p.212 Courtesy of The Well / p.213-215 Courtesy of Savoy Palace / p.216-217 Courtesy of Octant Furnas / p.218 Courtesy of Palacio Estoril, Golf & Wellness / p.219-221 Courtesy of Six Senses Douro Valley / p.222 Courtesy of SHA Wellness / p.223 Courtesy of Six Senses Ibiza / p.224 Courtesy of Kosta Boda Art Hotel / p.225 Courtesy of Loka Brunn / p.226-227 Courtesy of Burgenstock Resort Lake Lucerne / p.228 Courtesy of Grand Resort Bad Ragaz / p.229-231 Courtesy of The Dolder Grand / p.232-233 Courtesy of The Tschuggen Collection / p.234 Courtesy of Paul Massey / p.235 Courtesy of Corinthia London / p.236 Courtesy of Coworth Park / p.237 Courtesy of YTL Hotels / p.238 Courtesy of The Lanesborough Club & Spa / p.239 Courtesy of YTL Hotels / p.240 Courtesy of Gwinganna / p.241-243 Courtesy of Longitude 131 / p.244-245 Courtesy of Spa Qualia / p.246-247 Courtesy of Jean-Michel Cousteau Resort, Fiji / p.248 Courtesy of Intercontinental Bora Bora Resort & Thalasso Spa / p.249-251 Courtesy of The Brando / p.252-253 Courtesy of Aro-Ha

In the same series

Colophon

Text
Devorah Lev-Tov

Book Design
ASB (Atelier Sven Beirnaert)

Type setting
Keppie & Keppie

Back Cover Image
Courtesy of Anantara Kihavah Maldives Villas

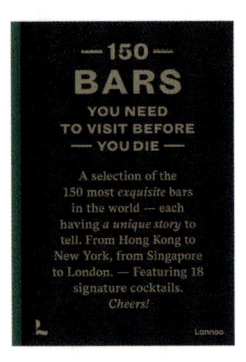

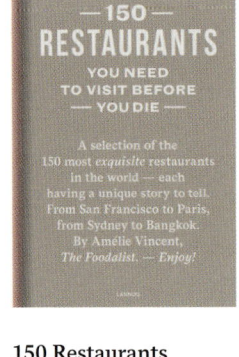

150 Bars
You Need to Visit
Before You Die
ISBN 9789401486194

150 Restaurants
You Need to Visit
Before You Die
ISBN 9789401454421

Sign up for our newsletter with news about
new and forthcoming publications on art,
interior design, food & travel, photography and
fashion as well as exclusive offers and events.
If you have any questions or comments about
the material in this book, please do not hesitate
to contact our editorial team: art@lannoo.com

© Lannoo Publishers, Belgium, 2024
D/2024/45/124 - NUR 450/500
ISBN 978-94-014-9747-3

www.lannoo.com

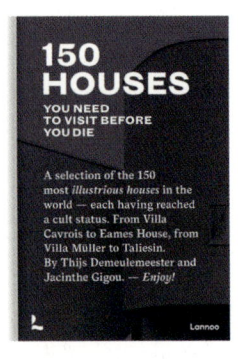

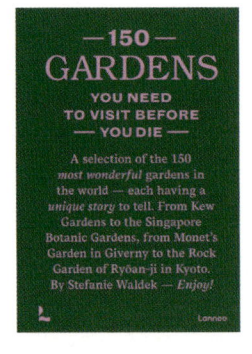

150 Houses
You Need to Visit
Before You Die
ISBN 9789401462044

150 Gardens
You Need to Visit
Before You Die
ISBN 9789401479295

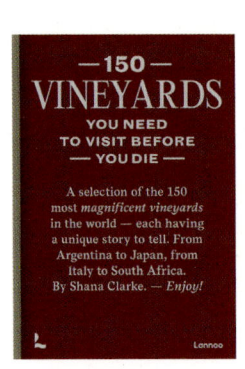

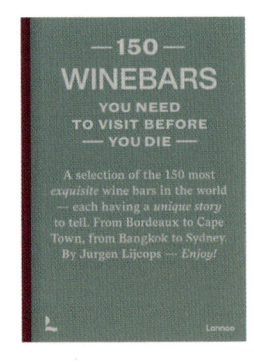

150 Golf Courses
You Need to Visit
Before You Die
ISBN 9789401481953

150 Vineyards
You Need to Visit
Before You Die
ISBN 9789401485463

150 Bookstores
You Need to Visit
Before You Die
ISBN 9789401489355

150 Wine bars
You Need to Visit
Before You Die
ISBN 9789401486224